Clear Boundaries

Every Business Woman's
Essential Safety Guide

Jessica Peterson and
Christine Beckwith

20/20 VISION PRESS

Clear Boundaries/ Jessica Peterson and Christine Beckwith — First edition
20/20 Vision Press, an imprint of Manifest Publishing
ISBN 978-1944913373

DEDICATION

This book is dedicated to all women who have encountered situations that were not safe in their business, whether online, at work, in business meetings, traveling, at home, or anywhere.

This book is further dedicated to victims of violent crime. During the writing of this book, Christine's coworker Colleen Brownell was murdered, on December 30th, 2017. Colleen lives on in the hearts of every person who worked with her and now, through the pages of this book her life and the many contributions she made are memorialized. May she rest in peace knowing she is missed and will not be forgotten.

This book is for you, your sisters and wives, your daughters and your mothers, for your employees and your colleagues.

"Risky business: Real estate agent's killing hits home for Realtors"

This headline told the story of Real Estate Agent, Beverly Carter—Murdered by a man who did not know her but knew that brokers were a target easily lured into meeting alone with strangers.

The publicity around the Carter murder signaled a change for real estate professionals. It shone a light on their safety, indeed on the safety of all saleswomen. Hundreds of stories have since emerged of assault and murder.

Reports and statistics show women to be **four times** more likely to be killed by homicide in work related deaths as compared to men. 90% of murders are perpetrated by men. That is a staggering statistic.

How many times in your life has the hair on the back of your neck stood up? How many times has your privacy been violated, your feelings offended, your respect undignified or worse have you been completely physically violated?

It has been our discovery in doing research for this book, in polling our female coworkers and women at large that there really are no women who have not felt one or more of the feelings we describe. Furthermore, women have been living silently, for the most part, with these assaults for decades, afraid of repercussions, afraid of their perpetrators, or just plain ashamed and humiliated. But, in the now famous words of Oprah Winfrey, "A new day is on the horizon."

In fact, the power that the recent movement has stirred is unprecedented and while you will repeatedly hear in this book that this has not been written about the movement, it will completely be impossible to not address the violations in general, to give you safety tips, that are part of the movement itself. That said, what we love about this book is that it's a forward answer, an offensive move, a taking back of power and a preventive sword for women. Instead of sadly looking in a mirror that has long since plagued all women, they are clearly looking down the road with the steering wheel firmly in hand.

So, we want to celebrate what our futures hold, how this newfound education will empower us to feel safer and quite literally be safer. How this book will save lives and be shared with peers and employers and churches and even young girls who need to understand and know how to protect themselves when in danger. By setting ourselves down a path to safety we hope that it feels progressive, healing, and positive. It is a challenging task to write a book that leaves out emotion and sadness when talking about violations of a sexual or physical nature. We believe *Clear Boundaries* succeeds in moving past the pathos and brings in its place a sense of liberation and unity, community, and strength.

Women tip the scale as the higher populated gender in the business workforce in 2017, with a 53% in their gender bucket. For women like Beverly and the many women prior and since, and those who today are in danger, we present this book. Please read and apply the safety tips. Please share the knowledge and the book. Let's change the numbers and prevent senseless violence and death.

Foreword

With over 50 years involved in First Response as a Law Enforcement Officer and Sex Crime Investigator, Paramedic and Firefighter, and now as a practicing Psychotherapist, I have seen the injury and eventual physical and emotional damage that is done to lives from a moment of inattention.

When Jessica Peterson told me about the book she was co-authoring, she expressed a goal that caught my interest immediately. I have followed the progress of this book, *Clear Boundaries*. And now that it has been completed, I truly believe Jessica and her co-author Christine will achieve their goal: I believe this book will absolutely save at least one life.

What do you say to a 75-year-old woman who was raped at 15 and never spoke of it? Can you imagine how this unfathomable event for a child has haunted the adult woman for 60 years? *Clear Boundaries* cannot take back 60 years of pain, but it can help give life back to the 15-year-old who is raped today and more to the point, give life going forward to the business woman who reads the stories and tips in this book and takes action to avoid danger.

Clear Boundaries is the perfect primer to assist women on how NOT to be a statistic in this systemic problem. The stories depicted in this book are a great start to making women, from young to more mature, aware of the signs and clues that a potential crime may occur.

All women must learn to trust their second brain (their GUT) to stay safe. As with any learning, these skills must be practiced daily to become second nature and a useful safety tool to eliminate danger before it happens. I would encourage everyone who reads this book to practice and teach others, including your own children (boys and girls), to help them set *Clear Boundaries.*

I look forward to reading the stories of the many women who will step up and share their own stories of trauma survived and valued advice in the next edition of *Clear Boundaries.*

Edward Rupert MA. PhDc

Emergency Responder Trauma Counselors

About Ed

"Be strong enough to stand alone, smart enough to know when you need help, and brave enough to ask for it."

This is the tagline for Emergency Responder Trauma Counselors (http://ertcus.com/), a practice founded by Edward Rupert. It defines the philosophy borne out of fifty years of experience with (and as) first responders. It also signifies why Jessica Peterson considers Ed to be "one of the few in this world with his extraordinary level of training and experience around safety."

Ed has been awarded the prestigious Red Cross of Hutt for his lifelong humanitarian efforts. He is an author, speaker, and educator who spent 13 years as a Police Officer in the Air National Guard, and continued his law Enforcement career with the Schaumburg, Illinois Police Department, and then The Larimer County Sheriff Department in Colorado as a Patrol, K-9 Officer and an Investigator of Narcotics and Juvenile and Sex Crimes.

Ed also worked as an Ambulance Paramedic while still involved in Law Enforcement. He was one of the co-founders of The International Association of Dive Rescue Specialists and is the co-founder of Larimer County Dive Rescue. Ed has also spent a 23-year career as a Public Safety Chief, developing creative and integrated approaches to industrial Firefighting, Law Enforcement, and EMS for a Political Subdivision in the State of Colorado.

Ed has served on the Advisory Board of a Safehouse for Domestic Violence Survivors and currently serves as a board member of the Poudre Valley Fire Protection District.

www.BusinessWomansSafety.com
Apple Iphone - SOS

Contents

Jessica's Thoughts 1

Christine's Thoughts 3

How Did We Get Here? 5

    The Real Story: Hotel Safety 13

Top Safety Tips 17

    The Real Story: Too Physical 25

Social Media Safety 27

    The Real Story: Stranger Danger 39

Travel Protection 43

    The Real Story: Travel Safety 57

Corporate Safety 59

    The Real Story: Listen to Your Gut 63

What Men Are Thinking... and Saying 67

    The Real Story: Personal Safety 73

Advice from an Executive Bodyguard 75

    The Real Story: Out at Night 81

Home Protection 85

    The Real Story: Professional Safety 93

Avoid Being a Victim 95

    The Real Story: Travel Safety 97

At the Heart of the Matter 103

    The Real Story: Office Safety 105

Realtor Safety 107

    The Real Story: Personal Safety 115

Keep it Professional 117

The Real Story: Violation of Trust 119

Taking the *Bull* out of Bullying..121

The Real Story: It's Not Your Fault...125

Closing Remarks.. 129

The Gift of Safety 133

Jessica's Thoughts

It Pays to Listen to Intuition

The thought of safety for business women kept coming up in my head. I was growing my agency, making a super positive difference utilizing my skills as a certified business coach in addition to managing my marketing firm for over five years. When people used to ask me who I am, I would say I am a Connector, Supporter and Protector. Business women safety was not part of my current plan but kept coming into my mind. Reminds me of the saying to listen to messages and your true calling.

Christine came into my life for a reason; to keep women safe. We originally met for a completely different reason; to discuss her being a speaker on an online show. As we started talking, she opened up about her passion to protect women.

No way! I manifested this woman to come into my life. This was a definite answer to my thoughts. I must, need, and will act on it!

We have a calling to educate business women on safety. Yes, I realize we are unable to cover every single scenario. If you have a scary moment and would like to share safety tips, please do connect with us. Our goal is to continue our education for women at our website www.businesswomansafety.com. Highly recommend you go there now and put in your name. We will notify you of any new safety tips that could keep you safe!

Christine and I have experienced quite a few different safety-related situations. We are here to share them with you and deliver awareness of what can happen to you. Our goal is to PREVENT it from happening to you.

Safety for Business Women is now one of the subjects I speak about, in addition to Productivity, Business Planning, Sales, Networking and Social Media. You can check out a full list of training at www.simplywowagency.com. We believe it is simple. WOW people. Your Business Grows. You have a prosperous aka WOW life yourself.

———

Christine's Thoughts

It Pays to Keep the Faith

You never know when returning a message or phone call can change your life. That is exactly what happened with meeting Jessica Peterson. If you ever think you are alone in the world, that there is no other person like you, don't lose faith. Jessica's energy, professional drive, and conviction rivals my own and inspires me. In one conversation we knew why we had been brought together and here we are making it happen at a time it is needed and necessary!

For nearly three decades I have been a professional woman in a business setting, often traveling across the country. Over those years I have found myself in dangerous situations. I was fortunate to be given a women's travel safety training by my previous employer and it has, on more than one occasion, allowed me to protect myself.

I believe I am here today because I stayed alert and applied these simple safety techniques; I have saved myself from hurt and harm.

As time has passed the frequency, the occurrence, and the boldness of offenses have heightened not lessened. I find this reality alarming in a business society where political correctness has increased along with the demand on professionals to be more polished. We are left to ask ourselves why.

I share facts in this book that help us all understand how we got here. And, with Jessica's research and true stories shared by professional women across America, we tell you how we survived attacks and most importantly how to protect yourself in the scenarios where you are most likely to be in the greatest danger.

Our goal in writing this book is to save lives.

As a society of women protecting ourselves, we stand to create great awareness and a community of protection from potential dangers. We want to hear your stories and share your tips with women across the nation using technology to our advantage. To help each other we have created a web-based link that any of you can access and add your stories and tips for preventive help. Share your story, anonymously or not, using this link:

http://businesswomansafety.com/yourstory/

We want to create clear cut solutions for you to draw the line and create your boundaries. We believe we have done this with this book and that *Clear Boundaries* will be shared by employers across the nation as a guide to mitigate the new and blurred lines that exist (both in and out of the workplace) for women.

-1-

How Did We Get Here?

Decades, Maybe Centuries, of History...

To understand how we got here we must absorb a few facts about women in the work industry and our own evolution. We looked at statistics from the United States Equal Employment Opportunity Commission (EEOC). In these findings, the source data carried through this decade and proved the following:

1. Between 1966 and 2013, women's participation rates in the workforce increased from 31.5% to 48.7% (2013 EEO-1 Indicators report). In 2013 in the United States, 161 million women made up roughly 51% of the population.

2. Despite overall increases in participation rates for women in the occupations as officials, managers, and professionals, barriers to entry still exist. In 2013, women represented 53.2% of the Professionals, while they made up only 38.6% of the Officials and Managers.

3. Women continue to experience occupational segregation in nontraditional jobs. Women comprise 7.3% of craft workers, while the participation rate for women in Office and Clerical Work was considerably higher at 75.6%.

What does this research tell us?

Years ago, there were far fewer women in the professional workforce, which meant much less business and professional interaction between men and women. It is clear that with the increase of women in business and the professions, the higher percentage of women coming in contact with men in the workplace has an observable effect on the number of inappropriate interactions that occur, whether reported or not.

What else do we know? What does observation, experience, and simple common sense tell us?

We know that:

- More women in the workforce (along with fashion changes), impact image requirements for women. How women dress for work and for social networking can be a reflection of their ability to progress and succeed in business. The demand remains that women must meet a male-defined level of social status, and wardrobe choices count.

- Social Media interaction is unavoidable. Online profiles are created and followed at a fever pitch—be they private, professional, or dating. Interactions, both solicited and unsolicited, are milliseconds or several clicks away, bringing men and women in contact on a virtual level far more frequently than ever before. The boundary is blurred when it comes to safe use of social media, to the extent that the separation between personal and professional is increasingly difficult to define and control.

- Lines are equally blurry when it comes to how professional women are depicted as sexual icons, both in and out of the workplace. Viewing sexually explicit magazines, while certainly a private matter, can become public and problematic when the perceptions gained by such imagery are carried over into the workplace. For men, and in truth some women, there is confusion about how much is too much sexuality.

- It's time for women to make a clear statement of boundary, supported by action. This topic is delicate and heavily debated by both genders.

  Let's be clear. No woman deserves to be violated, no matter what image she chooses to project on social media, in the workplace, or in her personal life.

  AND women must be aware that, fair or not, their social media image and activity, their professional image, and their private image are brought into play. This dichotomy shows clearly in character testimony for legal cases and it is not defendable. If we as women wish to protect our character, we must do so by how we carry ourselves in life as well as in the workplace.

- Men take chances with their perceptions of women. We also know that the time has come for men to acknowledge and embrace the reality that dating, romantic gestures, physical advances, and even aggressive advances toward women in the workplace needs to be halted.

  Again, let's be clear, romance does blossom at the workplace. Many a great relationship, marriage, and family started when two single people who met in a business situation felt a spark and then fell in love. That kind of mutually consensual relationship is of course acceptable and of course we are on the side of Love!

  For married men, and those in committed relationships, or men who make unwelcome, unsolicited, or improper gestures towards women in the workplace, we say it's time for men to halt this behavior.

No Debate

The current sexual harassment and discrimination climate is not up for debate in this book. We are watching that battle unfold in the media, along with you. We do not wish to create a controversial publication. This book is about safety. Gender comes into play because we are women who have chosen to address our message primarily to women. And yet, there is no doubt that *safety is the responsibility of every person and is 100% gender neutral.*

Our goal is for men and women to better understand the lines of delineation in the workplace. We intend to arm women with tactics that can be used against predators. It is time for all of us to take responsibility for how we protect ourselves, our image, and our safety; both men and women!

Based on the statistics we've discovered in researching this book, some of which we've shared, the sheer number of women in the workplace is not going to change. It is up to us to take the necessary steps to protect ourselves.

It is no surprise that second and third generation women are rising up to say to men, "Time for change, boys!" and move on.

What we are experiencing is similar to what past generations experienced with race equality. Gender battles are leaving scars, begetting notable discussion, and evoking controversial feelings.

One interesting fact to consider from our research is the role ethnicity plays. It is notable that many other eastern hemisphere countries have far fewer women in the workplace. In those countries, there remains an ethnocentric inequality that places women far behind U.S. women; their populations still live with a belief that women are home caretakers and men are the breadwinners.

While these same beliefs can also still be found in our U.S. society, many second-generation men in the workplace hold changed beliefs, a recognition of sexual equality and an appreciation of a woman's ability to choose career *and* family. These are starkly different attitudes than the beliefs of their first-generation parents, who most often experienced a higher-powered man as the 'king of his castle' and by extension, the rightful leader in the business world.

Make no mistake, there is momentum behind the changing roles of women, and that is going to increase not decrease.

Grassroots change is happening. Historic events are happening like the *Me, Too* movement that led to Time Magazine naming the silence breakers their Person of the Year in 2017. The Author of the *Me, Too* movement, Tarana Burke, initially started this movement ten years ago, but it didn't catch fire until now.

How did we get here? By numbers. By incidents. By a growing social media that has blurred our dating and romance lines. By the historic actions of aggressive men and more recent actions of assertive women drawing a line in the sand.

Are We All in Agreement?

There are women who see this movement as media hype, blown out of proportion, and who have spoken out against it. It isn't hard to find women who disagree with the zealousness of other women.

Why? I suspect for a couple obvious reasons.

#1. They have had bad things happen to them and were not able to act to defend or fight. They reflect on their past and dwell on the injustice done to them. Every woman in America has had bad things happen to them. Many, out of fear of their jobs or retaliation or alienation, have not taken legal action and won't. These women often resent those who speak up. At best, their heads are buried like an ostrich digging in the sand.

#2. They somehow can't relate to women who would risk it all to be a whistleblower when they have spent most of their career with the whistle in hand, but unable to blow it for the same reasons as stated in #1.

No, we are not all in agreement. We are, however, in the same place. What do we do now that we are here?

Can You Hear Me Now?

Women have been speaking up for a long time. And yet, much has been unspoken on both sides of the gender aisle.

Keep talking women, and more importantly, take action! Gift *Clear Boundaries* to friends and to coworkers. Share this with the men in your lives.

Companies have silenced the voices of women who point out the inequities and have ignored the issues for fear of financial impact. Companies are made up of people and this is an uncomfortable topic. We get it—you don't want to talk about it. And we don't accept that.

Companies, it is time to listen to your workforce and embrace the future. Truly, we applaud companies who have opened both their ears and their eyes.

To those companies newly awakened and to those struggling with accepting the new environment we say, "Share *Clear Boundaries* with your employees."

We want every book purchased to be held up in a selfie and added to social and professional sites with the words *Keep it Professional* as the caption.

We want every woman who reads this book to proclaim publicly that she is now certified in safety!

We want every woman to send out a message that you *will* act if a man violates space, privacy, or safety.

Clear Boundaries and our call to proclaim safety is not meant to scare men or incite riot. In these pages we describe a blueprint that leads to a clear line that cannot later be questioned, a line that defines personal space, privacy, and safety for women and makes it unmistakably clear where that line is and what will happen for men who knowingly cross the line.

This book was written to be a positive outlet and a forward movement on this front, to change the defensive posture of women who can't speak out or won't, to give women a guide to our future, and to guide them to choose how, in today's environment, they will act and react in their present and future interaction with men.

This is our contribution to forward motion and momentum in a positive light. This is a book companies can give to their employees to provide women support and protection. *Clear Boundaries* is tangible. It is NOT written from a politically correct point of view; rather it is a book that delivers real-life stories and practical solutions.

Women! *Clear Boundaries* is your future of safety, your future of protection in all scenarios. This book is born from the blood, sweat, and tears of decades of women who have been harmed.

Clear Boundaries is a gift for new generations of women entering and building the new world of professional careers. This is your book.

———

The Real Story: Hotel Safety

Which Floor Would You Like?

Suddenly, as the elevator doors close me in with this strange man, I realize I've seen him before. He is following me. His dazed and seemingly intoxicated eyes undress me as we make eye contact.

I know I block his view of the elevator buttons, so I ask him, "Which floor?"

He returns, "Same as you."

I know it is not a joke nor is he careful to hide his intentions. As the elevator rises to my floor, I shift gears into defensive mode. I ask myself, "Should I get off on my floor? I decide yes as the floor has already been chosen. My best course is to be, or appear to be, connected to someone. I reach into my purse and place my phone in my hand as the elevator stops and the doors open.

I step out.

He steps out behind me.

I turn left and start down the long hall where my room is the very last door.

He turns left behind me.

His steps, even on carpet, are loud to me; although not nearly as loud in my head as is the sound of my heart beating.

I begin a fake phone call, stridently saying, "Yes, I am walking to my room, I had a great night honey. How About You?"

I realize I cannot walk to my hotel door and open it. I am in trouble. I slow my pace as if distracted by my call.

His steps are louder. I feel him—too near, right behind me. He puts his hand on my shoulder, stops my forward movement.

I turn, pull away, take a step back. The phone is sticky with sweat still stuck tight to my ear. I say, "Can I help you?"

He looks stunned, angry, looks at my phone. He seems to register that we are not alone, that it is him, me, and whoever is on my phone. He demands, "Who are you talking to?"

I speak loudly to my imaginary caller, responding as if being asked about the man speaking to me. "I don't know, a man in the hallway is asking me a question." I cover the phone with my other hand, as if the man is interrupting me, and say, "Excuse me?"

He repeats, "Who are you talking to?" and he laughs out loud, a disgusted, angry laugh as if he knows I have thwarted his plan.

"My boyfriend," I say.

The man does not leave. He stands. Silent. Menacing. Perhaps confused. It is as if he cannot register what is happening.

This is my opening to escape. No way will I stand still while he plots his next move. I walk past him, toward the elevators.

The man says, "Where are you going?

Still holding the phone to my ear, I ignore him and engage in my fake call, talking actively. I walk rapidly back to the lobby and push the button to call the elevator.

He does not follow. Yet.

The elevator arrives, and I push myself through the barely opened doors, punching frantically at the close button. The doors take forever to open and then even longer before they begin to close.

I sneak a look out and I can see his shadow standing just beyond the edge of the wall, still following but apparently not willing to be seen. I am panicked at the thought he will jump into the elevator at the last minute.

Finally, the elevator lowers to the lobby. My hands shake violently. I am breathing fast and make an effort to calm my racing heart.

The doors open, I rush to the lobby desk, explain my situation. They look on their hotel cameras and see the man still standing where I left him. As they call hotel security, the man enters the stairwell and waits on the same floor.

Is he waiting for me to return, I wonder?

As security comes, and the story is explained, the man slowly makes his way down the stairs. As he nears the lobby, the security guard greets him, questioning him on whether he is staying at the hotel. The man flees out the side door, running away, never to be seen again. ~Christine Beckwith

Reaction and Response

From Christine:

Sadly, this story is not unusual. Women are followed all the time from bars and restaurants, but especially from hotel bars, which was the case in this story example. This is a real story. This happened in the past 12 months in Mount Laurel, New Jersey during a business trip. The unidentified man was a patron of the hotel bar.

In hindsight, I recall the man being at the bar for most of the evening. I had joined coworkers at the bar for a couple hours. I do not remember ever making eye contact with him in the bar, but I do recall his presence. He blended in, he was dressed in a business suit, collared shirt and sports jacket. He had not acted in any way that would have drawn attention to himself. He was at the bar drinking.

I am a traveling business woman. I have traveled for the better part of the past 20 years. Somewhere in my early years of travel I was given a course on travel safety. That course has always stuck with me and I have used many of the tactics that were taught, which have lent to literally saving me in very dangerous situations.

This event was shared with you to prepare you for what might happen to you or someone you love. What would you have done in this situation? What precautions would you have taken? Can you think of anything you would have done differently?

One simple precaution anyone can take is to turn around. Avoid going to your room if you see a person in your hallway. Another is to avoid getting on the elevator heading to room floors when it is just you and a man. I've been told that it was wise for me to pretend to be on the phone. Would you want to be even more prepared and carry pepper spray or a whistle? One of the best tip we've heard is to be confident and make eye contact.

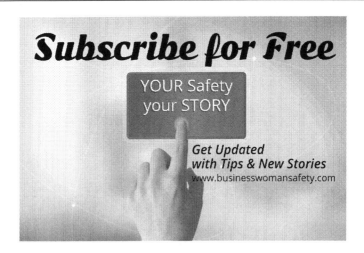

-2-

Top Safety Tips

Five Times the Protection with Top Five Survival Tips

E ach chapter in this safety book dives into specific scenarios where women are at risk or most likely to come into dangerous situations. We focus on the unique challenges and risks found in these scenarios, and share tips from a wide range of sources, including medical professionals, real business women in the workplace who are brave enough to share their stories, and professionals in the world of security and safety. In this chapter, the focus is general knowledge and five common sense arenas in which to practice safe habits.

Be Alert—Ready to Fight—Run, Loudly!—Prevent—Protect

#1: Be Alert and Aware!

Have you ever driven into your driveway at home only to realize that you were on auto pilot the whole way and barely remember any part of the drive? Whether you are at work, on the road, on the train, or simply walking across a parking lot, be in the moment.

The simple practice of mindfully bringing your eyesight for danger to top of your mind makes you more prepared than an unaware woman who is naïve about potential danger.

It is vital when moving around in the public, no matter what time of day or where, that you are cognizant. Be aware of your ability to move safely from your vehicle to a store, office, or building of any kind, and back. The term most often used by professionals for this is *situational awareness,* which is a fancy way of saying stay in the moment and alert to what is happening around you at all times. Don't answer the phone. Don't check your Facebook feed. Make it your goal to appreciate and be connected to the place where you are, physically, rather than thinking ahead to the dozen tasks waiting for your attention.

Abductions occur at the greatest percentage in parking lots or as a drive-by abduction when women walk or run on the side of the road. Be aware of large vehicles that have more than one person in them. Often if not taken by gun point, a second perpetrator will grab you from a side door of the vehicle while the driver whisks you away.

Listen to your intuition. We are genetically programmed to be aware of and react to danger. Even when we are not consciously aware, our mind will alert us. Have you ever felt uneasy or uncomfortable for no apparent reason? If we listen and take time to evaluate what is causing red flags to go off in our unconscious, our intuition is a powerful tool to avoid danger.

#2: Fight for Your Life!

Most professionals advise that fight is not the first response women should take. And while we don't disagree, we believe that in women, the fight-or-flight response is more heavily weighted to flight, which makes it vital to prepare beforehand. Mindset preparation is as important as physical preparation when it comes to being ready, with only seconds of warning, to fight.

There are documented instances in abductions where the victim has escaped by pretending to befriend her captor—yet these scenarios are the exception not the rule. In a violent attack or abduction, you must be ready and able to fight—without pausing to think about how to do it. In later chapters, we share defense tactics, including tips given by professional defense experts.

Women who fight when attacked survive at a far higher rate than those who go along out of fear. This is contrary to scenarios commonly seen in the movies where the victim holds on for a full two hours by going along with the captor, then escaping unharmed to tell a story of miraculous survival. That kind of fiction makes a good movie, but the truth is that fighting immediately, loudly and blatantly, offers the greatest chance for survival.

We want you to practice a fight-back roleplay in your own mind to get used to it. It is vital you not freeze in a moment of danger out of fear, or a lack of knowledge.

#3: Run!

Your chances of survival increase dramatically if you can thwart the criminal act at the start and escape. Your chances of being violated or killed go up dramatically if you are put into a vehicle.

Do NOT listen to a criminal tell you that you will not be hurt if you remain quiet. That is a lie. That is an attempt to get your cooperation.

It is normal to be afraid, especially if the attacker is holding a weapon Our best advice is to take any chance to run. And make a LOT of noise while doing it.

"When I was 12 years old and walking home alone, one night just before 9 pm I was grabbed from behind by a masked man who was hidden in the bushes in front of an empty house. The police later told me that I was lucky. I screamed. Loudly and repeatedly. The man stopped dragging me toward his parked car and instead threw me to the ground. The police said that most people when attacked by surprise say nothing. The man

was not afraid of me, he was afraid of being caught and I made enough noise that everyone on the street heard. My father met me at the corner, baseball bat in hand, having heard me screaming for my Daddy's help from a block away."

~ Anonymous, Entrepreneur from Pennsylvania

A Phone App That Could Save Your Life

One of the latest updates in 2017 for Apple iphone users was the addition of the SOS alert system. Apple added this feature so that no human fumbling for help has to unlock a phone via passcode, expending crucial and precious time in a crisis. Any iphone user can make their cry for emergency help PLUS track their location. The instructions below come directly from an Apple article that is available online. https://support.apple.com/en-us/HT208076

When you use the SOS alert, your iphone automatically calls the local emergency number, based on where you and the phone are physically located at that time. In some countries and regions, you might need to choose the service that you need. For example, in China you can choose police, fire, or ambulance. You can also add emergency contacts.

After an emergency call ends, your iPhone alerts the emergency contacts stored in your phone with a text message, unless you choose to cancel. Your iPhone sends them your current location and, for a period of time after you enter SOS mode, it sends updates to your emergency contacts when your location changes.

Here's how it works

Call emergency services on iPhone X, iPhone 8, or iPhone 8 Plus:

1. Press and hold the side button and one of the Volume buttons until the Emergency SOS slider appears.
2. Drag the Emergency SOS slider to call emergency services. If you continue to hold down the side button and Volume button, instead of dragging the slider, a countdown begins and

an alert sounds. If you hold down the buttons until the countdown ends, your iPhone calls emergency services.

Here's how to make the call on iPhone 7 or earlier:

1. Rapidly press the side button five times. The Emergency SOS slider will appear. (In India, you press the button three times, then your iPhone automatically calls emergency services.)

2. Drag the Emergency SOS slider to call emergency services.

After the call ends, your iPhone sends your Emergency contacts a text message with your current location, unless you choose to cancel.

  o   If Location Service is off, it will temporarily turn on.

  o   If your location changes, your contacts get an update, and you get a notification about 10 minutes later.

  o   To stop the updates, tap the status bar and select, Stop Sharing Emergency Location. If you keep sharing, you'll get a reminder to stop every 4 hours for 24 hours.

If you use the Emergency SOS shortcut, you need to enter your passcode to re-enable Touch ID, even if you don't complete a call to emergency services.

#4: Your Internet Activity Matters!

The internet is a window into your life and the lives of the people you know as well as people you are not even aware of. Your internet activity and actions can give away personal facts to would-be criminals, like where you live, even if you don't list your home address.

Even pictures you post can be used to learn facts about you that you may not want shared. Images can give locations and it's often accidental or without your knowledge. The picture might be GPS tagged, a person could save your image and if your smartphone's location tracker is turned on, that image saved in another person phone can provide a location.

And what about your children and other family members? Yes, their internet usage is giving away the same personal information about themselves, and by inference, more about you.

In the social media section of this book, we are going to cover many of the ways that the internet can set the stage for crimes and become unsafe. We know that following our tips for safe internet use will help every woman be safer. In addition, we will share a way to let all men know that you will protect yourself and are not looking for unsolicited romantic advances.

The key to safe internet usage is to maintain a reasonable level of both security and privacy. Going offline is not a viable option for most (if not all) of us. Pay attention to the security settings that your social media offers and choose the level that fits your comfort and your technical skill with computers and other digital devices. Pay attention to who you invite into your social media world—and the spheres your family habituate.

#5: Image Protection!

Your IMAGE must project a person who does not welcome violators. Your image is your choice. Should you consider how others perceive your choice? That also is your choice. We offer suggestions in later chapters about image and what may be communicated to others. In this section, let's talk about safety tips and how image is used against victimized women in the courts.

That said, *there is no such thing as a permission slip for unsolicited advances.*

Image control is a growing concern and one that has been brought into the courts of law. Character attacks on victims are a defense used by predators. Projection of how a victim acted prior to an assault is used to mitigate actions taken by the perpetrator of the crime.

We do not condone violence against women regardless of lifestyle choice, image projected, or moral character. The message we share is one of protection—specifically this: *Women! Protect your image! Tone up your image before it can be used against you. There is no better person do so. There is no other person who will live with the consequences if image is used against you.*

It's common sense. A positive, professional public image avoids and controls misunderstanding in business, no matter what your profession, or your gender.

What about the image we choose to share for social or dating sites? In theory, personal and professional are separate. After all, the guidelines of sites such as LinkedIn clearly intend users to stick with professional use only. Even subtle flirting is inappropriate for business sites such as LinkedIn.

However, when it comes to image perception, the lines are blurred between professional, dating, and personal. Fair or not, dating images are brought into courtrooms to present arguments that blame women victims. Mindful decisions must be made about online profiles and the image you offer, no matter the purpose of the site.

> *"I was proud of how all my effort to get in shape and be healthy paid off. I posted images that, to me, were a simple documentation of my journey. I deeply regret that now. The pictures revealed more than I realized, and my pose was not ideal. Now I can't get rid of those pictures. They keep popping back up and causing issues for my family and in my work."*
>
> *~ Anonymous Real Estate Agent and Mother, Florida*

We offer a tool in the next chapter (*Keep it Professional* frame!) that anyone can use to minimize misperceptions over image. It is up to us to project the image we want the public to consume and then deal with the attention we receive when we cast that net. While we know solicitations will still occur with no provocation, we believe there is much we can do to control and minimize the effects.

———

The Real Story: Too Physical

Serious Creep Vibe

This gentleman I met and who I see at a regular networking event gives off a serious 'creep' vibe to me, and other women.

I first noticed when he would shake my hand every time I met him. Then other women noticed it, too. He does the same thing to all of us. When he shakes a woman's hand, he takes her hand and grabs the back of her elbow with his opposing hand.

It's a very physical act and uncomfortable. He gives off an impression of being attracted to the woman—and not in a pleasant way.

~ Anonymous Business Woman with a Networking Complaint

Reaction and Response

From the Authors:

Clearly there is no right or wrong response here. How would you handle this man? Obviously, he is a part of the business community and perhaps someone who cannot be completely avoided, which complicates choosing an appropriate response.

Perhaps the ideal advice is to be upfront and transparent. Give him a CLEAR, firm, and polite response. Pull away from his gesture and let him know that the extra physical contact is not appreciated. Perhaps say something about changing his habit of grabbing your elbow. It will be necessary to be direct and polite in what you say.

What did the woman who related this story decide to do? She felt comfortable taking these options:

1. First option was to ask him nicely what does it mean when he touches the elbow with a handshake?
2. The other option was to say she is a germ freak and would prefer a fist bump.

Subscribe for Free

YOUR Safety
your STORY

Want to share your story?
businesswomansafety.com/yourstory

Social Media Safety

How we Connect as People is Blurred

Never has it been more important to protect ourselves from violations made by men who have lived in a seemingly boundary less society. Over two decades of growing online and media interaction, as well as a growing pornographic industry and a dismissive society, the lines of privacy have blurred. These lines are distorted today. Damage has been done in the evolution of online technology where there is much confusion between personal and private space and dating and courting space. It is up to women to create boundaries in all areas of life by clearly drawing the lines. We believe it will require a movement to define these boundaries in a fair and definitive way.

Our desire is to create a movement by having women post a *Stamp of Protection* clearly in their online profiles and signatures.

Have you seen, and perhaps used, the fun frames that Facebook allows users to wrap around their profile pictures? Some frames are purely for fun and others depict a serious social or political leaning. Ours is intended to show support for and help create the *Clear Boundaries Stamp of Protection* movement.

You can find this frame on Facebook by clicking on your profile image and selecting *add frame*. Search the keywords, *Keep it Professional*.

Facebook will automatically merge your current profile picture with the frame.

Once you have updated your profile and see the frame wrapped around your picture, take a screenshot or save the image. This will allow you to use the framed image and upload it to other social media platforms you use (and that allow such personalization). Thank you for helping us help you create *Clear Boundaries* in your life.

How to Avoid Misleading

Where do we begin in Social Media to create the boundaries we desire? Perhaps by first acknowledging that it is your responsibility to define your professional persona and your private one.

What if you are a single lady who wants to attract men who may want to date you? How do you protect yourself and still present a public image that is attractive? In our opinion, there are three different personas to consider: Determine what is personal, what is professional, and what is dating.

As more and more people use social media, and as social media plays a broader role in our lives, it is increasingly important that each of us control our image and public projection and decide, based upon the intended use of the site, how to project that image.

We suggest that both men and women keep romantic interaction to dating sites that are clearly meant for that reason. Even in the dating world we recognize that the boundaries and depths of deviance span a wide spectrum.

Use all social media sites as intended. We do not expect social media sites created for business to define boundaries for how members use the sites for romance. This responsibility falls on the member, on you.

None of us attended an etiquette school for social media. The rapid evolution and extent of technology interaction in our lives is alarming. We are defining the rules, making mistakes, and learning best practices at the same time, young and old alike.

Even five years ago, few could predict that every image passed between phones would forever be locked in a world of public exposure. Our world is one where hackers breach privacy on a massive, global level in attacks against seemingly secure companies and institutions.

In a truly fascinating article (*From Attire to Assault: Clothing, Objectification, and De-humanization—A Possible Prelude to Sexual Violence?),* author Bhuvanesh Awasthi explores the neuroscience of how human brains perceive objectification and violence. He cites studies that point to the role played by external cues such as appearance and attire, and identifies common threads such as clothing, sexual objectification, body perception, dehumanization, and assault.

As part of his findings, the article states, "Sexual violence is a consequence of a dehumanized perception of female bodies that aggressors acquire through their exposure and interpretation of objectified body images."

Let's pare that down a bit. Sexualized women are perceived as less competent and less fully human. Sexual violence happens because exposure to the female body desensitizes and dehumanizes women. That's a global statement, and we fully realize that this is a complicated subject. Yet, neuroscience is clearly showing that when it comes to image, perception of that image does count. If you'd like to read the entire article, you can find it at this link. It's freely available.

https://www.ncbi.nlm.nih.gov/pmc/articles/PMC5344900/

Why, we wonder, are people (and in particular young women), not concerned about the images they post and share?

This is a subject which is confusing and controversial even among women. Jessica is an entrepreneur and a social media expert, a wife, and the mother of a young daughter. She is also one of the authors of this book and she shares these insights:

First of all, and most important, no matter how a woman or anyone dresses should ever be reason to do harm.

I remember reading an article many years ago that talked about criminals who, looking for easy prey at the gym, preferred to target women wearing loose clothing because it was easier to rip the clothes off. I'm not saying that wearing tight or loose clothing is the answer. Each of us must make our own decision.

My point it, we should love and respect all people no matter how they dress. I grew up with one conservative parent and another who was not, which opened my eyes to how differently people think and how different they can be in personality as well.

Recently, a social media friend (Jim Deal) posed these two questions in a discussion I started about image perception and how women choose to dress. I found my own answers to be illuminating and suggest that you also answer these, according to our own intents:

1. What are women seeking by the way they dress?

2. What do women think men are thinking about the way they dress?

What I valued most is that these questions, especially the first one, made me think about my image and my preconceptions. Be honest in answering the questions and consider asking a trusted man to give his perception of you in response to question two.

Jim's response on my social media post continued as he shared the following: "My daughter used to do body building competition and some swimsuit modeling.

*When she got some honest feedback from some guy
friends, she was grossed out and stopped. Regardless of
your view of genders, men and women are wired differently. Women offer sex (not necessarily literally but sex
appeal) for attention and men give attention for sex. I
know that may be oversimplified and a general statement (and some folks might not like it), but from my
observation this is more the case than not. As usual,
there are always exceptions to any rule."*

Are we as a culture becoming sensitized to provocative images?
That certainly may be part of the issue. Internet porn is a billion-
dollar business and online webcam interactive porn sites have become frequented activity for men. When a lady simply looking for a
boyfriend, for a companion, posts a sexy-looking profile picture on a
dating site, do the men viewing that image expect to see (or be invited to send) nude photos? Is that image permission to the male
viewers to offer unwanted solicitation?

When women use social media sites as dating sites, we become
part of the problem by blurring the lines many of us are working to
clarify. Sexually explicit photos are not beneficial to any of us.

It is easy to see how the lines are blurred. In Victorian times, a
glimpse of an ankle was considered provocative. In some modern cultures, images of a woman's hair are considered sexually explicit. It is
clear that choosing to present an appropriate online presence will
continue to be challenging for men and women as long as the boundaries and the very definition of provocative is not clear.

Women have a responsibility to behave in a manner that is condu-
cive to the sites purposes. How a woman dresses and whether it
matters should not be a controversial subject. It is wrong to assume.
We are not here to judge anyone.

Be part of the solution. When you see a woman clearly misusing
social media sites to solicit men on non-dating sites, report her just

as you might a man. Pictures of a sexual nature on social media, no matter who posted, are against the rules of most sites.

Take a stance. Help us draw clear boundaries. It starts at home. Take responsibility for your image online. Be aware of the consequences to yourself and to others when lines are blurred.

Unsolicited Sexual or Romantic Contact

Christine shared this message string, posted recently on one of her professional sites:

Unknown Man:
Hey Christine
You have sexy look

Christine:
This is not a dating site!
Thank you for the compliment
Have a nice day.

Same to you.
I know but if we want we can make lot of fun here
By the way you are very rude
I am angry to you

This is not a dating site.
It's a professional site.
Sorry. I didn't mean to be rude.

its ok but Can I see you nude
i am sorry its a direct question
hilo you there?
Just want to f**k
Your a$$hole
i think you are out of control
i am sorry if you mind

While the perpetrator will remain anonymous, Christine reported this person to her company's human resources and to the professional site she was using. Christine clearly made it known that this was an unsolicited, unwelcome, and improper exchange. We must protect ourselves. Being clear with our intentions is not enough.

Make it a Movement

Social media has great power to create change and spread a movement with unparalleled speed and rapidity. We propose to use this power. Will you join us?

What if your profiles had a symbol that this man and every other man knows as a symbol meaning that you will act against him if he violates the clear and defining line of acceptable behavior?

We have such a symbol. Please join us in using the *Keep it Professional* frame in your social media and other public profiles where such statements are permitted.

It's time we stop presenting a defensive posture and give ourselves permission and the tools to join the offensive team. Let's take this movement on and leave no one guessing where we intend to be, leave no one uncertain about the fact that we are serious about our ability to protect ourselves. It must start with us. We must stop misleading men and instead educate and lead with clarity.

General Social Media Safety Tips

1. Be clear on how you use each social media site you visit and in which you participate. On sites where you do not want dating or solicitations from men, and when the site allows such a display, please clearly show the stamp of protection *Keep it Professional* picture frame.
2. Do not post sexually explicit phots of yourself on sites not intended for dating.

3. Be clear about your intent and stay professional, especially on your business sites.

4. Be direct in your response to unsolicited dating advances of a romantic nature.

5. Report immediately any unsolicited advances of a violent nature to both your employer and the site management. All chat lines on social media have a report button and many of them have additional options to file an abuse report.

6. Keep a record of the reporting the person and offense. Save a screenshot if possible.

7. Block the person immediately or remove them from your social circle.

8. We've mentioned this previously, and it bears repeating. Be careful when posting pictures that you do not give away your location in the process.

9. Do not overlook the obvious. Avoid posting your actual home address anywhere on the internet, on your own social media sites, or posting pictures that give away obvious locations. More and more criminal activities happen because the victim unknowingly tells the criminal where they are by posting.

Safety Tips for LinkedIn

Viveka von Rosen with Vengresso and a Forbes Top 50 Business Women, is a well-known LinkedIn expert and power user. We are grateful to Viveka for providing these tips. Even if you are not a LinkedIn user, the practical advice is useful for anyone who frequents social media sites for business.

LinkedIn, in my humble opinion, is one of the most powerful tools for women in business. And like all social platforms, it comes with risks. I'd like to address some of those risks, and solutions that women in business can implement to make their own choice about how to use this powerful business platform.

1. Never connect to anyone you don't want to.

2. If you happen to connect to someone by mistake, (or who seemed OK at first) you can always disconnect them. If they are bad, you can block them. If they are really bad—you can block and report them!

   To disconnect someone, simply go to their profile, click on the *more* tab under their name, and choose *Remove Connection*. Also use this tab for block and report. And keep in mind that you do not have to be connected to block people! Block and report is available to any LinkedIn user, regardless of connection status.

3. You can make yourself anonymous on LinkedIn. If you want to do research on who the people engaging with you are but don't want them to see, go to your settings, and choose the *anonymous private* option under the *privacy* tab. Or follow this link:

   https://www.linkedin.com/psettings/profile-visibility

4. You control how visible your profile is. If you are un-comfortable with the idea of your profile being fully visible to everyone in the world, use your privacy set-tings to make your profile visible to only *your network*, or only *your connections*, or only *people on LinkedIn*, or *everybody*. Even if you make your profile visible to everybody, you can still choose which elements of your profile to share. Under *Settings > Privacy*, click on *Edit your Public Profile*. Or follow this link:

   https://www.linkedin.com/public-profile/settings

5. Control your privacy setting for connections. If you are uncomfortable with people seeing who you are con-

nected to on LinkedIn, adjust your privacy settings so that only you see your connections. In *Settings > Privacy*, click *Who Can See your Connections*. Or follow this link:

https://www.linkedin.com/psettings/connections-visibility

6. Control your image. If you are uncomfortable with people seeing your picture, you can hide it from anyone who is not a connection. If you are hoping to network and grow your business with LinkedIn, it is both important to control your image and to show your image. And it must be a likeness of you, according to LinkedIn user agreement. If you put a logo up instead of an image of you, LinkedIn could limit your account.

One way to drive engagement on LinkedIn is to share content. Once in a while you get a creeper who abuses his or her right to be on LinkedIn. About a year ago I did an article on equal pay.

https://www.linkedin.com/pulse/87-cents-dollar-seriously-viveka-von-rosen/?trk=mp-reader-card

It went viral, and I got hundreds of responses. Many people had their own opinions, which is fine. What was not fine were the responses from a couple of men who were downright abusive.

You don't have to take that! You can block anyone who comments on your articles and updates. Not only that, but you can report them if they are extremely abusive.

There was one person who was completely out of line, and his comment on my article was beyond disgusting! I'll spare you the details; it's enough to recognize that he was on a business platform, using his real name, and his profile—which is attached to his company—saying sexist, racist, and crude remarks. A friend of mine, equally disgusted by his comment, reached out to the president of his company. She shared the comment—which was public—with this guy's company president, who ended up firing the guy. *There are consequences for abuse on a public forum!*

When you state an opinion that is completely against your company's public policy, and you share it on a business platform, you could suffer similar consequences! I just wish I had thought to report him.

Don't let the possibility that idiots like him could connect with you. You control your success on LinkedIn. There are many ways you can keep yourself safe, visible, and secure on LinkedIn!

Aimee

The Real Story: Stranger Danger

Tips for Staying Alert

I travel and speak at women's groups, conferences, events, and associations in every industry and can tell you from experience that there is no age or occupation limit when it comes to safety for women. This is something that we have to practice, regardless of whether we are grown business women experienced in our profession or young women venturing into the world of independence and career for the first time. Never let yourself be lulled into a false sense of security, even when you are with people you know and like.

Most of the time incidents happen when nobody else is around. One of our best defenses is ensuring that there is another person present to bear witness.

One especially memorable, and scary, incident happened to me when I was traveling. I entered the elevator, and a man followed me in. This truly happens often, yet something did not feel right about this guy from the minute I laid eyes on him. Even so, I wasn't really alarmed. There was nothing overly menacing about him.

When I hit my button for the floor, he stated that he was going to the same floor. This is when I felt my intuition alarms go off. My internal alarm sounded strongly, and I listened!

I busied myself rummaging in my purse to avoid conversation and just before we reached our floor, I said, "Oh, I forgot something in the lobby." I did not get off and rode the elevator back down to the lobby where I asked the desk clerk for an escort back to my room.

I do not know if this man had criminal intent or for that matter any wrong intentions, but his intent is irrelevant. The point is to be alert and listen to warnings even if there's no obvious threat.

To this day, I am convinced that by paying attention to my intuition and acting upon it, I kept myself safe and got out of a potentially bad situation.

~ Aimee Cohen, Founder & CEO WomanUp!
Keynote Speaker, Career Coach & Best-selling Author

Reaction and Response

From Aimee:

Tip #1: Have an elevated sense of awareness verses fear. Be aware of your surroundings. Be professionally and situationally aware.

What if you travel alone? Do your best to ensure you are around others and not alone when not in your room. Most of the time incidents happen when nobody else is there. You want someone present to bear witness. When traveling, ask to be on the same floor at a hotel with people you trust.

Of course, when someone breaks into your hotel room, you call hotel management and security. What if it is a coworker who makes unwelcome advances or attempts to get into your hotel room? In addition to the hotel security, do you know who to call at work? What resources does your company have available to you both while you are away and once you return? Be prepared. Learn your options before you travel.

What if you are at a networking event? Have a fallback plan to exit a conversation if you feel uncomfortable. Listen to your intuition. What action can you take? I've used some of these exit excuses:

- "You have been so generous with your time, I no longer want to take up more."
- "My goal was to meet five people. Great to meet you!"
- "I see a friend of mine or the speaker and I am going to say hello. So, please excuse me."

Are you going out socializing for work or with coworkers? Enjoy the event and maintain your professional face. This is when defenses are down. Everyone wants to be nice, get along and have no conflict when socializing. It's easy to have a false sense of security when you are with people you know and like. Nobody wants misunderstandings and uninvited advances to be the fallout after an office social event. Watch your alcohol consumption. Many companies encourage alcohol free parties for good-reason.

Tip # 2: Speak Out! What do we do after an uncomfortable event has happened, or an unwelcome advance has been made? In the story I've recounted, the man was a stranger to me. We teach our children to shout Stranger Danger, and had that seemed appropriate, I would have yelled!

Yet, in real life it's not always the stranger we need be concerned about. Consider how much more often the true risk lies with someone we know. When the danger comes from a coworker, or worse someone in a position of power over you like your boss, it becomes uncomfortable or difficult to avoid seeing and interacting with them.

Don't avoid them! Reclaim your power. There is no reason to hide. Be direct and act normally. Make them uncomfortable, not yourself.

Tell your story to get support. Confide in a friend at work. This friend can be your second eyes for safety to watch out for you and cheer you on so that you can hold your power.

From Jessica:

You will see Aimee speaking at conferences, associations, corporations especially niched in construction, finance, architect, banking, and more! Her hot topics include Playing Office Politics Like a Pro, It's all Workable: Resolving Conflicts with Confidence, and Movin' On and Movin' Up...Top Tips for a Successful Job Search.

Travel Protection

Stay Safe Out There

This is one of the most dangerous times for women to be defensive minded. Travel can be scary if you are not armed with the knowledge to keep yourself safe.

Last year, Christine undertook a nationwide 18 city road show for her company. With a hectic schedule, she was on red eye and late-night flights that put her alone in rental cars in strange and unfamiliar cities driving in the dark. Staying aware of safety and her surroundings was vital.

> "In my travels for work I have found myself in cabs being driven in the wrong direction twice. That is not a bad statistic considering the extent of my travel. In both cases, had I not used an offensive move I knew would protect me, I believe I may have been driven into a dangerous situation. In both cases I am certain I was being taken somewhere other than where I asked to be taken. I am grateful that being alert, aware, and prepared allowed me to thwart these attempts."
>
> ~ Christine Beckwith

Where are the risks to be found when traveling? One obvious risk is often overlooked, perhaps because it is rarely an issue for a man. Those who engage in heavy alcohol intake lower their inhibitions, their alertness and their guard against solicitation. This is when the greatest danger for a woman exists; this is what perpetrators watch and hope for. While it is perfectly acceptable for a man to relax all evening in the hotel bar—and no one has the right to fault a woman for doing the same—the risk for a woman is higher than for a man.

Yet another blurred line.

Is a woman 'asking for it' if she acts a manner that some consider unladylike? The debate on this subject is wide and emotional. Are women mentally are prepared to close the deal on a romantic advance when, or if, the boundary lines are blurred by heavy flirting in which she participated? Many court cases are thrown out as unwinnable if even a hint of complicity and consent can be shown. We've already mentioned the trend to use pictures and the sexually explicit appearing activities from social media in the defense of perpetrators against women.

It's no longer a matter of social judgment alone. It's not a matter of being a good girl or wanton woman. It's a matter of being fully informed of the consequences and making educated decisions when it comes to risking your safety today and in the future.

There's more at stake than simply being driven by a taxi driver in the wrong direction due to lack of geographical knowledge. Let's discuss how to protect yourself in these and more travel situations.

Airports & Airport Transportation

The greatest risk for travel safety at airports is being followed into parking lots, or away from airports, by a stranger who is watching you unknowingly and/or a person who has friended you and invited you to meet after the airport.

Here are our best safety tips for these situations:

1. Give yourself plenty of time when departing to find a decent well-lit parking area.

2. Do not enter dark parking lots alone. If entering car parking garages, make sure you are in a well-lit area. The trick here is to pay attention to where you decide to park.

3. Make sure you remember your parking spot. Roaming around parking lots or spending more time than you should in a parking lot and acting as if lost can give a perpetrator time to approach you, follow you, or act as if they want to help you.

4. If it is offered as a legitimate, advertised service of the facility, not a private vendor, take advantage of shuttle transport directly to your car.

5. Under NO circumstances should you accept a ride in a car to help find your car even if it's extremely cold and you are not dressed for it. Ask the facility's security staff for assistance if you cannot safely travel outside due to weather.

6. Take a photo of where you are parked and note floor and section as well. Refer to your photo to get back to the parking spot in the most seamless way.

7. Never let an attendant in the rental car or parking garage offer to drive you anywhere even if across the parking lot. There is never a need for an attendant to be in the vehicle with you.

8. Take no shortcuts through non-public or protected areas in the airport. These areas may be unstaffed and may not be visible to security, are poorly lit, and are not monitored for public protection.

If taking ground transportation once you have arrived, there are two simple steps you can take to ensure your safety once you enter your transportation vehicle. Think about how easy these steps are:

1. Ask the driver for his name.

2. Make a call to a friend and say, *"I am in a taxi headed to X (give exact location) and am in cab #12345678 with Ralph."*

Be sure to give time and trip duration, *"It's 7 pm and we should be at the hotel by 7:20 and I will call you again once there."*

You can fake this call if necessary, leave a message at another number, or even call your own home phone, and leave a voicemail message to yourself. This anchors you to safety. This is a truly simple and effective safety practice. It works.

Do not discount this tip because it seems too easy or basic. When a driver knows you have told someone you are with him, he also knows that any crime committed will be tied to him.

If using a limousine service, make sure it comes with a credible online rating and safety rating. Look them up under Better Business Bureau and be sure they are a legitimate service.

"I was taken by a paid limo service off the route to my home from an airport and then the limo driver pulled over and said there was a flat. I could see a gas station in walking distance, but the neighborhood was not the best, and I was uncomfortable. I was uncertain what to do, so I called a friend who advised I get out of the limo, take my bags and walk to the gas station to wait. My friend stayed on the phone with me the whole time until she got there."

~ Anonymous Traveler

Never allow yourself to be put in a situation where you could be at a disadvantage.

Hotel

1. Beware of dark parking garages. Park your rental car in a well-lit area. Walk straight from car to entry.
2. When possible, use valet services to have your bags checked at the door, then park the car. Avoid whenever possible being encumbered with luggage when walking back.

3. If you have no choice but to park a long distance from the entry, use a hand-held flashlight, or the embedded smartphone flashlight to light your own way to the entry. By doing so, you are then able to be seen by hotel guests in their rooms and other observers in any area around you. That is also vital to your own safety. Perpetrators are more likely to take you if you are walking in the dark and not seen.
4. Be observant when dining or having a beverage at the hotel bar that you do not engage in conversation with someone you can't trust.
5. Be aware when you enter the hotel elevator that you never get in with just one other person who you fear could be following you. In fact, get off the elevator as if acting like you forgot something at the front desk if you need to.
6. If you fear you are being followed in a hotel, immediately take out your phone and act as if you are speaking. Even better, call someone for real.
7. Never open your hotel room door if you are in a hallway with a guest who is acting like they may be watching for you to enter your room. Wait to enter in privacy even if it means waiting by the elevators until the other guest is in their room.
8. Never allow a repairman or bellman in your room with the door shut, keep the door open always when service is being provided.
9. Make sure when entering and exiting your room that your door is safely locked behind you either way. Hotel doors are heavy, and many times will rest but not lock without a push.
10. Check your room upon arrival to be certain closets and bathrooms are unoccupied.
11. At night, make sure your cell phone is in reach, on the nightstand, on the bed under the pillow. And make sure it's charged! Make sure you have easy access to a lamp without getting out of bed, and that you understand an exit plan or

strategy should your room be entered by anyone with a hotel key, like a manager or hotel employee.

12. Never give your hotel room number out to anyone that you do not trust, obviously. Conceal the wrap where the hotel number is written for the keys you get and put it in your notes section of your smartphone if need be.

13. Get two keys upon hotel check in and put each in a different place. In case you lose one, you will not be stuck for a long period in the hallway. Standing in front of a door fumbling and searching for a key is an unsafe place to be and carries a high potential to be grabbed and pulled into another room.

General Travel Safety Tips:

1. Do not leave your purse unattended during travel where someone can gain access to your hotel keys.

2. Do not drink to intoxication if you are unable to care for yourself safely.

3. Do not give your hotel information to anyone untrustworthy including work mates.

4. Do not leave your drinks open when in the bathroom, always put a napkin over your drink. It's far less likely your drink would get drugged if you take this simple step.

From a Corporate Traveler

Cynthia Beyer is an attorney, speaker, and author. She shares lessons learned while with a company that had an excellent travel safety program for their traveling female executives.

Several years ago, I had a job at an engineering company. Literally within the first week, a cross-country business trip was scheduled. Previously, my business trips had been in-state, in Colorado. This trip was going to be to Atlanta, Georgia for an extended time. This was not traveling to a local conference for a day; this was a new level of travel for me.

One of the mantras at our company was *Safety First*. The mentality to be safe first rather than getting the work done was novel to me as well and one I appreciated in this company.

Having traveled across the world, I did not think, these business trips would be any different, but they were. During this project, our entire team learned many lessons about how to travel safely.

The first lesson and not the least was to appreciate the power of following a routine and knowing how our own needs fit a general flow of travel. Do the logistics of getting from point A to point B shown here resemble your own routine?

...Check in for the flight.

...Go through airport security.

...Walk to the gate.

...Board the plane.

...Fly to destination, arrive, and deplane.

...Get the bags.

...Find the location of the rental car place and rent it.

...Hop into rental car and drive to the hotel.

...Check in to the hotel.

...Collapse on the bed and try to sleep.

As simple and ordinary as this flow appears, in between are potential missteps that can and do occur to impact safety each time we travel.

Before your next trip, think about and evaluate your own routine travel flow to identify points where your safety could be impacted. For example, I have a friend who travels with wheelchair assistance. The greatest potential for danger to her lies in getting into the airport terminal and then again getting on and off the plane. Everywhere else, the logistics are controlled by transport personnel who accompany her between gates and throughout the terminal.

I have taken the lessons learned over the course of the many travel trips and created this list of safety tips:

1. Learn how to pack light and effectively. Use carry-on luggage when possible to avoid waiting at the luggage carousel.

2. When sitting in the plane, count the seats to the exit row. If an accident occurs on the plane, the cabin fills with smoke, you want to be able to count up or back from your seat to exit the plane safely. Or better yet, be in the exit row so you know how to get out. Also, when they do the safety talk at the beginning of the flight, listen to them. Those five minutes might be difference between life and death in an emergency.

3. Keep your shoes on during the flight. Remember the scene in the movie *Castaway* where Tom Hanks is the bathroom when the plane explosion hits. He does not have his shoes on and eventually he lands on the island with only his socks. Point is you never know when you may need to exit and who wants to be looking for your shoes.

4. Check your rental car. When you pick up your rental car, look it over. Does it have any scratches or marks that need to be marked down? Does it have its side mirrors? How about a spare tire? One of my colleagues on a trip, got a flat tire. When he looked in the truck to get the spare out, there was not a spare. Same thing holds when you return the car, circle it and make sure you don't have damage. You could have been side swiped in the hotel parking lot and did

not realize it until you are turning the car in. Consider taking pictures to preserve the condition of the vehicle. Those extra minutes taken to protect yourself may also save you money and time later on by not having to explain yourself.

5. When you get to your hotel room, also look for the exit to the stairs and count the doors on how to get out. Again, if smoke fills the hotel, you don't want to stumble around while getting out.

6. Lock your hotel room doors. Entrance and balcony! Also, check the locks on the windows and any adjoining rooms. If it has a double bolt, lock both.

7. As you prepare for bed, have clothes and shoes nearby that you can put on in case of an emergency at the hotel. If you need to leave the hotel in a hurry, everything is close by. Have a small flashlight that you bring along. If the lights are out, you can find your way with it.

8. For single ladies, have you ever thought about wearing a cheap wedding band? It may stop some guys at the bar from stalking you, especially if you look single. A ring may not stop some from hitting on you, but it may be a deterrent.

9. Use your peephole on the door. If you have someone knocking and you did not order room service, you may not want to open the door to strangers.

10. If you go out for dinner, let someone know. Then check in with them when you get back. Do you want to be the body that goes missing for days before people start to look for you?

For the Frequent Traveler

Ava Diamond is a world traveler and a speaker on leadership and women's success topics. She travels the U.S. and globally to present her programs and usually travels alone. These are travel safety tips she's sharing from her own experience and research.

- Research the area you'll be traveling to. Know where the dangerous areas are, and plan to stay away from them.
- Give your itinerary and contact numbers to key people in your life. Place copies of your itinerary in each piece of checked baggage. Take a photo of the exterior of your checked bag, and of your packed suitcase.
- Your luggage tag should have only your name and cell phone number. You could also add your email address. Do not put your home address on the tag.
- Leave your valuable jewelry at home.
- Pack a portable charger for your phone. You want to be able to use your phone at all times. Keep it in your purse or backpack. Have your ICE (in case of emergency) numbers stored in your phone.
- If there is a distraction in a public place, grab and hold of +your purse or other bags. Often, distractions are used as an opportunity for pickpockets to take your items.
- If you are out walking, make sure you have your business card or ID on your person or in your shoe. In case of emergency, you can be identified.
- Don't sit in a car by yourself looking at your phone. If you do, lock the doors and be in a place with lots of people. Don't park in a dark place far away from your destination.
- When sitting at a café, make sure your purse is away from passersby, not on the floor next to you or hung on your seat.
- Lock your car doors when driving.

- If you must ask for directions, approach women with children. To add another level of safety, say you are meeting your husband there.
- If you go into an airport parking garage late at night, ask for airport security to go with you. They will expect to be tipped.

International Travel Tips

- Research the customs and the culture of your destination country. Know the appropriate dress and behavior, both for your business meetings and for your time off.
- Check out any U.S. State Department advisories. Enroll in Smart Traveler Enrollment Program (STEP) U.S. Department of State https://step.state.gov/step/ STEP will send you important information about safety conditions in your destination country and will enable you to stay in touch with the U.S. Embassy. If you decide not to enroll, at least take the embassy's phone number.
- In a country where your phone will not work, you can get a disposable cell phone with a local number or get a local sim card installed in your own phone. Give the number to the concierge, and to your trusted family members or friend. Make sure you write down the number.
- Take a few hotel business cards with you. It will be helpful for taxi drivers, particularly if you are in another country.
- Make physical and digital copies of your passport and visas. It's helpful to have a photo in your cell phone as well as stored in the cloud. Leave a copy of your id or passport hidden in the pocket of a piece of clothing or tucked away under the lining of your luggage. This way if your purse is lost or stolen, you'll have a copy of your ID immediately available.
- Don't use stand-alone ATMs. Ones inside banks are safer, and less prone to identity theft. Use a wallet with RIFD security.

- Stay on well-lit streets at night, and well-populated streets during the day.
- Walk with confidence. If you have to check a map, do it before you leave, or duck into a store or restaurant. Don't check your map on the street.
- Keep your head up and your eyes looking where you are going. Don't have your eyes glued to your phone or be listening to your headphones which makes you less aware of what's going on around you.

Air Travel

- To prevent blood clots on long flights, flex and point your feet often, and get up and move at least every two hours. Wear compression socks on long flights. They make a difference.
- Instead of storing your carry on directly overhead, place it over the seat in front of you and across the aisle. That way, you can have an eye on your things.
- If you go the restroom, take your purse or your wallet.
- Consider pre-arranging airport transportation to take you to your destination. This can save a lot of hassle, especially if you are in another country and don't speak the language.

At the Hotel

- If you are coming in at night, and there is a parking garage, call the front desk and ask for someone to escort you.
- Don't take a room on the first floor. It's best to be somewhere between the third and sixth floor. You want to be high enough that it's difficult to break in but within the reach of most fire truck ladders.
- Don't take a room next to a stairway. Criminals often use these for easy entry and exit. Don't accept a connecting room.
- Do not let the front desk clerk say your room number out loud. If they do, ask for another room. Ask the front desk

clerk what the number is to call in case of emergency. If your hotel is a large, spread out resort, don't be in an isolated location. Ask for a room in a building near the lobby.

- If you are having a bellman bring your luggage to the room, stand by the open door with tip in hand, and give it to them as they are leaving.
- Check the locks on windows and doors. If they are not functioning, call the front desk. Check the closet, the shower, and under the bed. Check for bedbugs.
- Identify your fire escape route. Know where the two nearest stairwells are. You want to avoid elevators in a fire.
- Keep your door locked at all times when in the room, including any additional deadbolts or security locks. Never prop your door open, even for a brief time.
- Tie a jingle bell to a ribbon and put it on your room door. An effective way to be alerted if someone tries to open the door.
- Use a simple rubber doorstop! Toss this dollar-store investment into your luggage and increase your security tenfold. Have you ever tried to open a door against one of those rubber stoppers, especially on carpet? It can be done but not silently and not quickly.
- If someone comes to your door unexpectedly claiming to be hotel staff, call the front desk and make sure a staff member has come to your room. Don't open the door until you are sure of who they are.
- When you leave the room, put the do not disturb sign on, and leave the television or radio on. It will look like your room is occupied. If you want housekeeping, let the front desk know.
- When leaving the hotel room, if there is someone in the hall, reopen your door and say loudly, "I'll be right back, John" to the empty room. It makes your room look occupied and makes it appear that you are not traveling alone.

- Use the in-room safe for your valuables. This might also include your electronics, anything with your home address on it, keys to your home, extra credit cards. If you are in another county, leave your passport in the safe and carry a copy. No in-room safe? Often the front desk can lock it up for you.
- If you get on the elevator and feel uncomfortable with someone in the elevator, get off the elevator and take another.
- If you order room service, and are traveling alone, don't leave your tray in the hallway. One glass and one plate tells passersby that you're by yourself. Call Dining and ask them to pick it up for you. Most hotels would prefer that, anyway!
- If you are traveling alone, make sure someone knows where you are headed for and when you expect to return. You can let the concierge or front desk know.

———

The Real Story: Travel Safety

Be Aware and Alert to Enjoy the Experience

"I would like to go out and take a power walk. What would be a safe route for me to take near the hotel?"

The woman behind the front desk at the Ritz Carlton in Jakarta looked at me like I was crazy.

She said, "I would recommend you do not leave the hotel by yourself. We have a workout facility with an outdoor fenced in walking path. You should walk there."

I explained that I had a male colleague coming in the next day, and that we'd like to tour the historic part of town.

She again recommended that we not leave the hotel.

That was really the first time I was thwarted from doing what I wanted to do when traveling.

~ Ava Diamond

Reaction and Response

From Ava Diamond:

Traveling the world, having new adventures, and experiencing other places and cultures will change your life. Don't let fear stop you. Take precautions, be safe. And be willing to go for it!

I have been forever changed by many of my travel experiences, both domestically and globally. Book the trip, savor each moment, and stay safe! Go in with a positive mindset, that each trip is the adventure of a lifetime, and that you are open to all that it will offer you.

–5–

Corporate Safety

"For never was a story of more woe than this of Juliet and her Romeo…"

Most Corporate safety issues occur either in a closed-door space or a social work setting. There are many things that can be done to set the stage properly for office place safety and it starts with the relationships that are formed within the workplace. It's vital that boundaries are defined in people's work lives.

Workplace romance happens. We are all for a great love story! Yet not all office relationships are romantic; not all are safe; not all are mutually desired. In this chapter, we address the less pleasing and unsolicited type of advances that could put a person in danger.

Not every man flirts and makes advances. The majority of interactions between men and women colleagues in the workplace are friendly and professional. Yet there are also far too many situations where the advances made are aggressive.

Here are scenarios that are most common:

- Workplace sexual advances
- Workplace sexual verbal statements, emails, or texts
- Workplace Social off-site settings

Our best advice is to avoid getting into these situations all together. Be clear. If you do not want to enter into a romantic situation, be clear with your voice and actions.

When comments are made or actions taken that you consider inappropriate, speak up and say that you do not welcome that type of relationship. When you define your boundaries there's less confusion and less opportunity for finger pointing later.

When you clearly say no, that you would rather they not do or say or act in a particular way, you are being respectful of them and of yourself. Everybody deserves person-to-person notification...

Once...

Assuming, of course, no harm was done. An insinuation, an invitation can be forgotten, when it's not repeated. Your precise statement communicates clearly and defines the future of the relationship.

What if you can't avoid it? What if you find yourself in a situation where unsolicited verbal or physical contact occurs without warning?

Stop the situation immediately, end the meeting, and seek a manager and safe environment, even if it means retreating to the nearest restroom. Once composure is restored, go directly to human resources to report the incident and notify your direct manager. Together you will plan for your future safety while they gather the needed details.

We have seen and been in a position to review many situations of this nature. The lines can easily be blurred. When clear boundaries were not drawn beforehand, wanting men have taken advantage of a door semi cracked open.

Whenever possible, deal directly and immediately with any circumstance that feels uncomfortably like an advance you don't want. A great tool for success to mitigate these kinds of slippery intersections is to use jest and humor. Suppose you were to say, "We don't want to cross some sort of line that would put both of us in an awkward future position, plus I want to run for President one day." Then laugh with as much sincerity as you can manage. This lightens an otherwise awkward moment. It allows for the coworker to step away, ego intact, and understand clearly that you have personal boundaries and want respect.

Corporate Safety must start with the proper policies and procedures, practices, and education from the top level down. That begins with ensuring a safe working environment a proper sexual harassment system and a firm response to any discretions.

Off-site Work Events

Many companies have travel or off-site events as part of their usual quarterly agenda. Depending on your position you may travel frequently for many reasons. Even those companies where travel is not part of the work, off site social events for the company such as company picnics or holiday parties can be a total nightmare for the amateur party goer.

It seems silly to have to recite to grown adults that their demeanor, even at an off-site event, is still reflective of their company's mission and of their own continued professional success. Yet, it needs to be said and reminded.

Movies have been written on this topic, often with a lot of humor injected. In today's environment, it is more vital than ever that both women and men present their absolute professional best in managing their boundaries.

Whenever alcohol is involved, it is especially likely for things to go badly. Be sure to understand your company's policy prior to getting into a situation that cannot be reversed later.

Proper attire comes to mind in this section. Many social events beg for fancy attire however it is important that all parties dress appropriately for the event and remain professional.

ANONYMOUS

The Real Story: Listen to Your Gut

A Close Call

I showed a house a few years ago to someone who found me through a website. The appointment was middle of the day. The house had a long driveway, was not close to neighbors, and was vacant.

We went inside. All seemed well until he started asking personal questions like whether I'm married, and what's my age. There was nothing sexual, but nothing about the house, either.

He was very built, was ex-military, and kept getting close. Too close. I started getting a strange vibe, so stood in the open doorway with my key between my fingers like a weapon. I told him to check out the other two levels on his own.

He came back to the foyer and asked me about something in the back of the house, wanting me to follow him there, which would have meant I had no way out. I responded to his question but wouldn't leave the doorway.

We went out to view the yard, and I stood near my car while he walked around because I was more and more uneasy.

When he was done, he told me he felt like I had rushed him out of the house, and I told him I was expected at another appointment. I gave him my card, and he stared at it a long time then commented on my picture.

The next day he texted to tell me how attractive I was and to ask about the house.

I had a bad feeling. Maybe I was paranoid, but I wasn't going to trap myself in with him. I don't wear heels unless I know the person now. I would have never been able to run.

~ Anonymous Real Estate Agent

Reaction and Response

From the Authors:

One of the best things we can do for ourselves is to maintain top of mind awareness and alertness to danger. As humans we do sense danger, but with civilization danger has become disguised and varied into many forms, many of which we do not immediately recognize.

One such form is in our business interactions. Just as we started this book with the dramatic headlines of a murdered real estate professional, we remind you all in this shared story above how meeting in any entrepreneurial way can be a dangerous proposition.

Meeting alone is no longer an ideal situation and when the risk is life and limb why risk it? No one will be offended if you have a peer partner around. Consider the risks in all you do.

Use a buddy system at all times. Meet during daylight hours. Always be aware of the exits in any building you enter and keep the closest exit in front of you.

Document the identity of the person with whom you are meeting. Write it down. Snap a picture of him or his ID with your smartphone. Send the ID documentation to the office immediately and while in his presence. Let him know what you are doing.

Listen to yourself. In personal meetings when men give off a sexual vibe, an attraction, and make it known in their words or their eyes, these are men who clearly you do not want to be with in a private space and in need of protection.

Make it known immediately if verbal compliments pass your *comfort zone*. Let it be known that vulgarity or romantic gestures are unwelcome and totally unacceptable.

Do not be afraid to report situations to your employers as well. They often have a plan to help you handle potentially difficult situations with grace, dignity, and support.

What Men Are Thinking... and Saying

A Male Perspective on Corporate Safety

Men want to know their boundaries. They would cross fewer lines, leave less open for interpretation or to others' discretion if they understood clear boundaries. From the male perspective, a lot of doors are left open by women.

Men are business owners, boss's friends, husbands, fathers, and brothers. They want to protect the women they love and admire. They want to run companies that are not put in liability or risk of legal action brought on by inappropriate behavior. And they are, like women, put in awkward positions to police activities that may lead to inappropriate situations in professional settings.

The Broad View

We need to be willing to look at the problems our society faces and open dialogs to address the issues.

In this book, we categorically state that safety is everyone's responsibility. Each person controls much of their individual safety zone by monitoring image, environment, situations, and even geographic location. Quite literally we control where we go, how we look, and who we surround ourselves with. Perhaps more to the point, we each control the lure of entanglements and intersections. Whether we engaged with or without permission on both sides, changing one's mind is a right reserved by all.

As we delve into the male (and in some instances the corporate) perspective, we ask you to keep an open mind as we may make statements to which you take exception. We are not debating society's issues. It is not our intent to begin an argument. And we absolutely do not place blame on women when lines are crossed by the men whose unwelcome advances have the power to change lives by violating privacy, protection, or safety. There are, simply, clear boundaries that are not meant to be broken.

Those boundaries, broken or otherwise, are the very essence of this books' intent. The boundaries we identify and define exist to help each of us mitigate the line, for both sides to understand the part they play in the social stigmas that are prevalent, and more importantly, for everyone to act in the workplace with the kind of dignity that protects all.

Workplace fun, humor, friendship, and comradery is not in jeopardy of being lost by professionals when it resides and is entered into in a non-violent and innocuous manner with no hidden agendas.

Companies can do everything they should to educate every single hire and still not give full protection in all situations. There will always be situations when a company must expend resources to investigate and mitigate claims. Women must decide if their rights are being violated; then act, respond to, and hold culpable the perpetrators—on a case-by-case basis.

This is why it's vital that we establish clear boundaries, that we act, and react according to laws and policies rather than emotion or disdain. It is in the best interest of any company, and employees at any level, for a company to create and implement a clear statement indicating their position on women's safety, sexual harassment, and sexual discrimination.

What the Men Think

We surveyed men in the professional field, asking them to give us three actions they thought were important to ensure that mixed signals were not being sent when men and women work together.

The top three answers from one Psychologist were: Poise and Pitch, Keep it Professional, and Know Your Purpose in Meetings. His words may raise an eyebrow. Please keep in mind that this is the male perspective and while you may not agree, he has a valid point of view and one that all should keep in mind for that reason.

Here are what he considers the top three behaviors and actions that men find confusing and that women have great power to control:

1. *Poise and Pitch.* Women need to carry themselves professionally and speak in a way that is professional. The pitch of a female voice can imply closeness to a man, even when it's not intended, which makes it important for women to develop and use a business voice in the workplace.

   Women are often blamed for sending mixed signals. It's hard to understand when a woman is flirtatious, for instance, then later squelches an advance as inappropriate. That's where poise becomes vital for a woman to maintain.

   It is important that both parties remain professional—in and out of the office. When friendships are formed, and professionalism relaxes, it can become difficult to understand the lines and where they are crossed if the parties are also socializing outside of work.

2. *Keep it professional! Don't get personal. Keep it Professional* and there will be NO confusion. *Keep it Professional* and you'll never give off the wrong signal.

Keep it Professional and no man will misinterpret your be-havior as an invitation. When she keeps it professional, he can't help but follow suit. The number one reason men give to explain away an interaction that they later discover was awkward or worse is the excuse that *she was asking for it* or *she was putting off a vibe of wanting my attention.*

3. *Know Your Purpose in Meetings.* Don't get distracted and go off topic. This point is about preparation. Going into professional settings knowing the plan and what points you intend to make leaves little room to be misunderstood.

Are Your Signals Mixed?

Consider your current behavior in the workplace Do you need to rethink any of your habits and practices when interacting with men at work to *Keep it professional?* Here are actions we've identified that men may find confusing:

- The topics women bring up in meetings.
- Discussion in one-on-one settings, or even in situations where they may be overheard.
- How women choose to dress in the office and at business events held both in and out of the office.
- How women choose to behave in professional interactions.
- How women talk about their boyfriends or husbands. (If you have one, mention him, he's part of your life, but consider carefully before you complain about your spouse or discuss your love life in the office.)

When in a Male-Dominated Career

This response is from Christine, one of the authors of this book. Over the course of her 30-year career, the majority of her col-leagues have been men. This includes peers and those who report to her as their manager. Her perspective is important in understanding how to relate to men in business.

I found that early on in my career I wanted to be taken more seriously than I was. Other women were leery of me, which at my young age I didn't understand. I now realize that my appearance gave women professionals concern. I was wearing tight suits and dressed to look like the women in the style magazines. Sadly, I totally missed the ball in this since my goal was *not* to accentuate my gender. I would often wear my hair slicked back and dress in monotone colors of black, white, and gray.

Men were looking at me in a certain way and there were times in the early days when I liked that. We all like attention of course. Eventually, we must decide as women if our desire to get that attention belongs in the workplace. I understood early on that I needed to work to gain the respect I wanted with both genders. To be taken seriously I had to display my working knowledge, present myself professionally, and keep it all in that lane.

I made a conscious choice at one point to stop unsolicited advances before they could even be made. At the first sign that my space was being violated, I made sure that they knew I operated with intelligence before emotion, had an understanding of my rights, and that I was a colleague worthy of respect.

A huge part of me needed to prove my abilities through results. This took time. It also required, to a certain degree, that I accept the inequity women deal with in business every day.

When I started to win sales awards and top the sales categories, male colleagues looked at me with respect not desire.

Women do not begin at the START line in most of the business world (and in truth, in society as well). We start much further back. We can't really change that overnight.

We can demand that we be seen and treated as equal once we reach the playing field. We can have policy and procedure to protect our rights. We can even have advocates around us and in work to help look out for those rights.

We can earn the respect of our colleagues, both male and female by being professional in our work environment. There are more good women AND men in our industry who desire to help us lead the charge. It's our choice to use our position and power wisely to effect change that ensures equality, fairness, and professional behavior are recognized and acknowledged as our strengths in the workplace.

ANONYMOUS

—

The Real Story: Personal Safety

Even Good Guys Can Turn Out to be Bad

At one time I worked in sales for a finance company. My role involved a lot of traveling. One of my first assignments was really intense. The company expected me to work around 70 plus hours a week. The pay was great but not worth it when I realized I had no life. I share this with you because I do believe being overworked impacted my thinking ability.

During one trip, when it came time to leave and head to the airport, a gentleman who worked in security offered to take me to the airport. I thought, "What a super nice guy, and he is in security, I should be safe!"

As we headed out, he had to stop by his house. He had me come in for a short moment. There were no lights on in the home and it was dark. He claimed power was out. Looking back, I think, yeah right!

The next thing I knew he got me in his bedroom and on his bed. I was in such disbelief to what was going on. I froze and let him do his thing.

I was in a completely different city and state, not knowing people. I was in a place where I had no idea of its location nor did I know what his plans were.

It was surreal. I just wanted it over, so I could get the hell out of there!

~ Anonymous Rape Victim, in Georgia

Reaction and Response

From Georgia Victim:

Here is what I want to share with other women.

1. Because someone is in security or any safety industry does not mean you should trust them.
2. Never, ever, get into a car with a guy unless it is a paid service and even then, be super careful and cautious.
3. Do not ever go into their home. They may play it off as no big deal. Never enter!

If I had not entered the home, who knows what would have happened? Could it have been even worse? I don't think about that. It is clear now what his plan was all along.

After getting off the flight, I barely recall what happened. I think I've erected a wall around that night. I think I spoke to someone, I remember saying, "I think I was just raped." I do believe I went to the doctor for it. It is such a blur and a moment I want erased from my life forever.

What I believe and say to you today is that if any blessing comes from that horrific experience, it is in my gratitude for this opportunity to share it in this book and help maybe one woman avoid a similar experience.

-7-

Advice from an Executive Bodyguard

In the Heat of the Moment

As interesting and thought-provoking as it is to consider the male and female perspectives and discuss the controversial issues around safety that we all face today, we are committed in this book to provide you with the absolute best tips and advice around safety that we can put together.

One of the men we polled happens to be an Executive Body Guard. He provided some amazing safety tips that, while common-sense, are simply not always obvious. Be prepared is the common theme.

Consider these top points that he wants to share with you.

1. *Know All Your Exits—Always.* It is vital when entering any building you know all your exits. Quickly assess your exit areas. Be sure to have direct access to them if need be. This is vital for physical attack protection and also emergency situations like fires. Most buildings have exits labeled and illuminated but not all. Be vigilant and make it a habit upon entering to look for the way out.

2. *Be on the Same Level When Talking to Someone.* Never purposely put yourself at a lower stature than the person to whom you are talking. Women are typically shorter than men, so there is an inherent disadvantage. For you to remain seated while the person you are addressing stands adds to your disadvantage. It is worse to stand down a step or at a lower level. Make a level, eye-to-eye connection if possible. If there is an eye level disadvantage that you cannot correct, widen your distance.

3. *Posture Counts.* Have a strong posture and stance. While this is good for you physically, having a strong stance is powerful body language that speaks to your confidence and may in and of itself deter a perpetrator.

4. *When on the Phone, Hold your Head Up.* Never look down or be unaware of your surroundings when making a phone call. Phone calls distract us from our environment and limit awareness. We tend to lean into our phones and turn our backs, especially in noisy situations. Keep in mind this position may leave you vulnerable for an attack.

5. *Need to React in Milliseconds.* Every person in an attack has milliseconds to react. It is vital to have a plan already in your mind. Preparation or anticipation can totally prepare you for situations when they arise. Most victims of attack will tell you they were taken by surprise.

6. *Leave an Arms Distance from Others.* Protect your space. Keep a distance between you and a stranger, man or woman. This vital both for sending a message and for deterring the silent messages men feel are sent by attractive women a*sking for it.* That distance you create will send, and help men to get, the correct message. More important, having a physical distance when around others allows you time to pull away or run away. Being able to run always gives you an advantage.

Be Prepared

What do you do when you find yourself physically threatened or under attack!? As much as we would like to be prepared for every situation, at some point any of us may find ourselves physically threatened. By that, we mean about to be attacked or being attacked. We want to arm you with real lifesaving tips on how to position yourself in social settings to avoid attack or the potential for attack.

Screaming Loudly

"Help! Stranger!"

Would you instantly look around for who was shouting if you heard this? Yes. Most would. And attackers know this. A woman's ability to thwart an abduction or violent attack will rest greatly on her ability to scare off an attacker. That must happen immediately. Most attacks will be planned and while the victim is caught off guard, the attacker knows exactly what to do, to disarm the victim or disable them. They will likely strike hardest at the start. It is vital that you alert anyone and everyone around you with sound.

We went to the source, prisoners currently serving time for violent, random attacks on women, and asked, "How can a woman stop an attack?" Their number one piece of advice: Avoid a fight. Get help. Scare your attacker off.

Be loud and yell for help with words, not just by screaming. Screams can be dismissed as squeals of laughter, they can be denied as a real problem. It's vital you use words like *Help!* and *Stranger!* or simply *Help me!* You also want to fight hardest while you are yelling and if you can get loose, run.

Makeshift Defense Weapons

Makeshift means you grab and use what is at hand. Even your jewelry can be a weapon. Jam that diamond into his eye if you can. Grab the ballpoint pen from your organizer to stab and tear at the soft tissue around his face and neck. Hairspray, mousse, even antimicrobial hand cleaner sprayed in the eyes will burn and perhaps delay the attacker long enough for you to get away or help to arrive in response to your shouts.

Keys can be used as a weapon if needed to gouge eyes or scratch. Place the key in the palm of your hand, as pictured here, so that the end is sticking out between your fingers. This turns your key into a makeshift defense weapon.

When you walk to your car alone, make it a habit to place your keys in your fist and hold firmly.

Be prepared. You want to strike to disable. Unfortunately for your attacker, you will go for their eyes or throat.

Keep in mind that you only attack in this way when you are in danger of or are being overpowered. Fight should only occur when you have no other way to get the physical attacker off you then do not hold back—your life may depend on you allowing your natural fight or flight instinct to kick into fight mode.

Get DNA

In the instance that you are being fully attacked it is vital that you scratch for DNA. Finding a runaway perpetrator will be far more likely and give you absolute peace of mind if you gather skin cells beneath your fingernails. Leave marks on the perpetrator that can later be seen by police investigators and that will provide vital DNA for an investigation team to examine. Your evidence can be entered into the law enforcement database systems to match a prior criminal and used to obtain a warrant of arrest.

Force and Power Defense Moves

Kicking as a defense

In a situation where you are being attacked you will want to use power and force. One of the ways women can use extreme power or force is by either kicking or grabbing and twisting. Kicking can take a person down, you want to kick at the side of the knee, so it buckles their stance.

Groin Kicks or Twisting

You also want to kick in the groin where it may also change the physical plans of the perpetrator and stop the sexual arouse at the same time. You can also grab and twist the scrotum forcefully. You want to make whatever defense move you make impactful.

Eye poking

You can scratch, gouge or poke eyes to disable a perpetrator. As mentioned previously, this is a particularly vulnerable place and injury here will stop someone in their tracks.

What are you Carrying?

Most women carry a purse or bag of some sort—and it likely weighs a few pounds. Swing it, don't drop it. Aim high for the face and eyes. If you can't get leverage for a high swing, aim low to buckle his knees. Remember, the side or back of the knee is vulnerable.

These days it might be a cell phone you carry. If it's in your hand, it can be swung. When it connects, it's harder than your hand and may provide distraction and that split second you need to escape. Aim for the temple, it's close to his eyes and may cause him to pull away. Something as small as a phone may not hurt, but in that split moment, the attacker may not know what you are holding, and the power of surprise is your advantage.

Do you walk with a cane? That is a weapon in an attack. Wield it, if you can stand without it. Use it to block blows. Use it to poke. Use it as a lever to break an attacker's hold.

Take Action

Bottom line, if you are being physically attacked, react! Fight, yell, and run. All at the same time if possible!

JESSICA MAC

———

The Real Story: Out at Night

Not a Halloween Trick

~ Shared story, a Facebook post from a friend of the victim.

Repost from a neighbor.

Sharing from a friend's post on Facebook. This incident happened last night, November 29th, in Parker to a woman in her mid-30s. While this was not in our neighborhood, everyone should be mindful of staying vigilant and trusting your gut.

I feel it's important to share what happened to me last night with all my friends as I normally don't post much about personal stuff, but I feel everyone needs to know that it can happen to anyone!

Last night was one of the scariest nights of my life, but my angels were clearly watching over me! I've never been one to be scared of going to the store after dark because I'm pretty aware of my surroundings and like everyone I just have to get stuff done.

I went to Michael's craft store in Parker at 8:30 pm. While I was in there, I felt as if two guys were following me. They didn't say anything but would go down the aisles I was in and one kept getting closer, too close for comfort. So, I decided to be done with my shopping and check out.

As I was walking out something told me to be aware, maybe because of the guys in the store or maybe because the parking lot is not well lit.

There weren't many cars in the parking lot and as I approached my car, I noticed a car being parked pretty close to my car but facing the opposite way so that my driver door was matching up to his driver door. As I was approaching my car, I saw a man sitting in the other car. He looked up at me and had a mask on kind of like a joker/clown mask.

Right when we made eye contact, he opened his door and pulled a gun on me. He was saying something under the mask, but I just started screaming as loud as I could and ran for my life back into the store.

He got away, and the police were there within a couple minutes. I'm not sure if he was going to rob me and take my car or take me, as sex trafficking is getting so bad and [we're] the #1 State for it. They still have not found him and there were no cameras in the parking lot.

The detective told me a similar experience happened in Castle Rock a few days ago and again in Parker off Strogh.

To all my dear female friends, PLEASE don't go anywhere by yourself after dark! Especially during the holidays. Always be aware of your surroundings and if you're walking in the dark to your car, make sure you have something to defend yourself!

I'm so glad I decided to scream and run and the police said that's the best thing I could've done. I don't want to hear of this happening to anyone else, so please share! God Bless and stay safe out there!

~ *Jessica Mac FB Share*

Reaction and Response

From the Authors:

What strikes me immediately about this story is that was shared on social media with local, geographic details. For all that we talk about the issues that come with technology's intrusion into our daily lives, this is a positive example of the how valuable social media is as a tool for getting the word out about a danger in one's own backyard.

There can be no doubt that the intent of masked men in a car backed in for quick exit was criminal. And this woman is to be congratulated for paying attention to her intuition which kept her on guard and observant.

Consider for a moment your own attention to detail on a routine trip to Michaels. Would you be alert enough to notice a car backed into the spot next to yours? To notice the mask on the man behind the wheel in time to run away?

Home Protection

Your Home Is Your Sanctuary

Christine has experienced three home invasions. It's hard to believe. The first was when she was 16 and home sick from school. The second happened in her first apartment, and finally in recent years again in a newly purchased home.

Perpetrators invading homes do so for two main reasons: theft and rape. Many times, criminals committing these acts are altered by drugs and alcohol.

Finding an uninvited person in your home, no matter what their intent or their mental state might be, is going to elicit a reaction from you. How you react may be the key to you, and your family surviving.

Your line of defense is a big deal. In reality, you must have multiple *Lines* of defense. We've identified several over the next few pages. Use those that make sense for you. Change and modify those that might fit your circumstances with a bit of creative thinking.

And add your own unique signature—the key is to prepare for a worst-case scenario, even if you never need to take even one of these defensive lines.

First Line of Home Defense: Security Signs

Does your home have a sign on the lawn or somewhere on the outside that shows a potential criminal that your home is equipped with a security system? If not, then it needs to be displayed.

When robbers were surveyed, they said the number one deterrent is fear that they will trip an alarm. Rapists are far more strategic on this front. When intent on reaching a victim, they will cut home lines to phone, electrical, and security systems. Signs will not deter them. The difference is often one of degree and intent. A robber seeks to steal stuff; a rapist seeks to perpetrate an act of violence. Even so, it is worth the small amount of effort it takes to display a *No Trespassing* sign or a *Beware of Dog* sign.

A sign does not mean you must have the security system or the dog. The point is, most thieves will not go to the trouble to confirm, they will assume you have the security if they see a sign.

Second Line of Defense: Security Systems

What happens when a robber or rapist gets to the door, window, or patio slider? Is it summer and your windows were left open at night? Did you run out to the corner market and leave the back door unlocked for your teenager who forgot his keys?

A home security system is one of the best lines of defense you have to call upon. It is, however, only as effective as you make it—a security system must be active to be effective. Bluntly, it must be turned on to protect you.

Set up your security system rules of behavior for family safety and follow them. Habitually.

- First floor windows should be alarmed, shut, and locked. Always, no matter the season or weather.
- Experts advise that your home security system be active at all times whether you are home or away. You want any attempt

to enter, at any time, to trigger the alarm. Minimum use (not recommended, but perhaps realistic for a busy family) should be to make sure it is turned on every you leave home. You do not want a potential robber or rapist to enter and hide.

- Subscribe to a security service that will trigger the silent alarm to the local police station.
- Pay attention to the upkeep of your security. Systems need to be maintained and checked frequently for active response.
- Internal cameras or motion detection cameras can be installed. Many security systems now have extra internal alarms that can be set at night, when you are home and sleeping, that puts motion detection security systems on the first floor to track movement and sound the alarm.

Dogs are great additional second line of defense They will alarm before your alarm will alarm. They will know when someone is on the lawn before they get to the door.

It was mid-winter and a fresh snow lay on the ground. That's how they tracked him—he left footprints in the snow and inside the house when he stood over me as I slept!

I had come in late from work and stopped at the store for groceries. Exhausted, I left everything on the kitchen table and lay down on the couch to catch my breath and rest—just for a minute. An hour or so later, I was awakened by my German Shepherd's intense barking. I wasn't alarmed immediately, but when my sleepy brain recognized there was a cold wind blowing across me and I realized my dog Buffy was barking from OUTSIDE, I was alarmed and afraid.

The police told me later that the dog likely saved me from something much worse than having my purse stolen. The thief's wet footprints were visible on the carpet leading into the room where I slept. He grabbed my purse and ran when the dog, who was sleeping at my feet on the couch, started chasing him. The invisible fence kept Buffy in the yard or I think she would have chased him down.

I was lucky. It was my own carelessness that allowed him to get into the house. The door was unlocked. It was a glass entrance and he could clearly see my purse open on the kitchen table. Kind of like putting cookies in a transparent cookie jar in reach of a 2-year old.

~ Anonymous, Medical Librarian in Pennsylvania

From Christine:

I love this story and the pet part. After my third home invasion, I put up a beware of dog sign even though I had no dog. Then I went out and got my first full size dog, who has added a layer of security for us like nothing else.

A dog truly can give you time to react. Those minutes are crucial. The pet you love may save your life. There are thousands of stories that prove this fact.

Third Line of Defense: Your plan.

Do you have a plan for how you would react in a home invasion? If you do not have a plan to react, fear takes over and many things can go wrong. It can happen anywhere and at any time and your family and you need a plan.

Ask yourself these questions and come up with answers!

1. What would you do if you woke in the middle of the night to the sound of splintering wood as a criminal is trying to break down a door with a crowbar?
2. Would you have enough time to get yourself and your children to a hidden space that protects you while you dial 911?
3. How many minutes do you have before police can arrive?
4. Where in your neighborhood would you and your children go if you had to flee your home?
5. What are your lines of defense?

Your answers to these five questions are your plan. Share the plan with your family members. Practice what you would do in an emergency, especially if there are kids in the home.

It is especially important to pay attention to question number five. Your third line of defense can save your and your family's lives if a criminal gains entry against all other defenses. Be certain that all family members know the plan and where to meet.

If you wake and you hear someone inside the home, you have seconds to react. Know your plan and be ready to implement

- An Attic or crawl space, a basement or closet that locks—these locations can be a place to run to, where you can lock yourself in and hide quietly. If you do this, leave lights off.
- Dial 911 immediately while in motion, every second counts. Simply state without many words that your home is being broken into, your address, and ask how long.
- Sit in silence keep 911 on the phone if possible.

We strongly suggest you sleep with a television on in one room. The sound of voices on a TV can deter a robber by implying that people are present and awake. That may scare off a thief who has entered the home. The TV sounds can also cover up sounds of you whispering into an emergency phone call.

Neighborhood Buddy Systems!

Have a friend in the neighborhood who has agreed to be your family's go to in an emergency, as a backup to 911. This person or family would receive a call AFTER 911. You may have a plan to do the same for your neighbor as a team.

Often, this backup person can be on-site before the police and can also make a second call to 911 to report the situation from an outside perspective. They can get into a vehicle, drive into the driveway and toot a horn, using car lights to make a perpetrator think the law has arrived.

We say this while suggesting extreme caution and recognizing that any safe activity that interrupts the act of a crime is an action to consider. This has been proven to halt an emergent crime in process and cause thwarted criminals to flee.

I once had someone try to break in. I was home alone and heard them start going to the doors and attempting to open each one. Thankfully, they were not successful in finding an unlocked door or any other way in.

I called 911. The sheriff came out. That day there had been a festival across the street from my home. The deputy's determined that the most likely suspect was someone who was at the festival and saw me walk home with my friend, who then left me alone.

The Sheriff suggested that I call some male friends to come stay with me that night. I was able to find someone but had not planned ahead.

It's important to have a buddy in mind who would come. Ask ahead of time, before there's an incident, so that your buddy knows how to get to you.

~ Anonymous in Colorado

Final Line of Home Defense: Weapons

This is a personal choice for all people. If you choose to have a weapon in your home for self-defense situations, we advise that you take extreme care to avoid the use of that weapon becoming tragic.

We strongly suggest that you:

- Are licensed in applicable states.
- Are trained on proper use of the weapon.
- Use weapons only in violent and clear threat to life situations
- Are trained to use your weapon as a disabler not a killer, meaning you can take a perpetrator down with a leg shot and avoid killing with a head or chest shot.

Most importantly, if you choose to have a home defense weapon, we ask that you keep it out of reach of children. Teach your children that they are NOT to touch said weapon. Put your weapon in a place where young children cannot access it at all.

As your children grow and you choose to train them in the use of the weapon, please ensure that your older children understand when to use it as well.

Finally, place the weapon in your *safety spot* where you run to in an extreme situation, that way it is handy only in dire situations.

Your home is your sanctuary. Unfortunately, sick and desperate people are out there, and the chances of violence have increased in recent years. Single women or single mothers are the greatest target for intelligent criminals who plot robberies and rape. If you fall into this category, it is vital you follow this home protection guide. It will help you.

———

The Real Story: Professional Safety

The Hot Chick

As a young business professional woman, I have worked hard to ensure people see me for my brain and the passion that I bring to my work. And it is something that I have been successful at.

However, one individual made my feelings of confidence shatter with three small words.

At a work conference a month after being hired to an internship, I was asked to assist in a presentation about a highly technical software product that I barely understood. Directly after the presentation I received positive feedback from my managers and team.

About two weeks later, the attendee feedback forms were sent out to the presenters and as I looked through, I saw an odd response: The Hot Chick. As I dug deeper, I found the question to which these words were the response: "What was the best part of the presentation?"

I instantly felt uncomfortable being in the office and around any of my male coworkers. I had no idea who had said that and felt a sense of violation.

My work mom, as I refer to her, was the only one I felt comfortable discussing the situation with. She was my advocate through the whole process that followed, one that resulted in meetings with third level management on what the course of action would be. My manager told me that there would be zero tolerance for that type of behavior, a response for which I remain grateful today.

~ Alyx Van Doren, Marketing professional

Reaction and Response

From Alyx:

Without the support of my manager, and his reassurance that the individual who made the comment would no longer be with the company, I would have continued to feel uncomfortable in my place of work. He was fired, and I became fully confident again at work. ☺

From a company standpoint, my advice to both young women and men in the workplace is to reinforce the understanding that unwanted sexual behavior and comments toward women is never okay.

On an individual level I encourage women to seek an advocate within their company. Develop relationships and advocates who you can use as a resource and become that resource for others in turn.

Avoid Being a Victim

Vehicle Protection

A common place for women to get attacked is at stop lights. Experts and the police tell us that women are often victims of men jumping into cars at lights and stop signs.

We tend to think of our car as a safe zone and to a certain degree, it is. Certainly, the ability to step on the gas and drive away to escape danger is a huge benefit. However, in a carjacking scenario the safe zone can become a deadly danger zone.

Do not be lulled into a false sense of security. Be alert, even in the relative safety of your car. Implement these vehicle safety tips into your daily routine:

- Always drive with doors locked.
- Never pull over when a man driving alongside points at your car like something is wrong. Drive to the nearest well-lit gas station and look the car over or ask an attendant.
- Never sit in an unlocked car—anywhere. When you pull over for any reason, keep the motor idling and the doors locked.
- In the event a door is opened, be ready to accelerate but not into danger. If you can move the vehicle do so and do so fast.
- Always have your mace or other defense weapon in the car.

- Be certain that your defense weapon is easily in your reach from the driver's seat.
- Consider keeping a duplicate of your preferred defense weapon out of sight and available from the back seat. Be certain to ensure that children cannot accidentally set it off, that they know it is there, and why.
- Don't park in the same spot every day for work. Criminals watch for that activity and plot their plans. Park randomly, and park in well-lit areas.

Car Break Down

It is sad that we are in a place as a society we must fear being a helpful person, but it's true. Don't stop to help the motorist with a flat tire. Instead, call 911 to report the broken-down vehicle. Be alert to the possibility of deception and provide help without putting yourself or your passengers at risk.

What if the shoe is on the other foot? What if it's YOU who are stuck on the side of the road in a break down or flat tire situation?

- Please do not open your car door to a man, even one in uniform. Crack your window and speak through the crack while you assess the person's credibility.
- Let them know that help has been called for even if it has not! Do not give the impression of vulnerability.
- Ask their name or if they live nearby, or why they are on that road. It's a red flag, and a good sign that the person has ill intent, if they don't give credible answers. Criminals will not give you information. They are creative about it and will slyly sidestep a direct answer to your question.

The Real Story: Travel Safety

Even Experienced Travelers Must Remain Vigilant and Situational Aware

I have been traveling the world for 40 years.

As a former military wife, I've traveled extensively around the world. Initially, I traveled alone with my small children. Then later in life, I traveled alone for my job.

Even before the terror attacks on September 11th, I always carried pepper spray in my purse or pocket. When I traveled, it was my habit to move the pepper spray from my purse to my pocket as I left the hotel or airport. After all, it is always challenging for a woman alone, or with children in tow, to get to a car parked in the lot of a hotel or airport while carrying purse and luggage. I felt safer knowing my pepper spray and phone were always in my pocket.

After 9/11 carrying pepper spray became more involved. I could still carry it in my purse at home, but when flying the pepper spray had to be placed in my checked baggage. This meant when I reached my destination, before leaving the airport I had to retrain myself and remember to open my luggage, take out my pepper spray, and place it in my pocket.

This is something I remembered to do ALMOST all the time. One of the few times I didn't, here is what happened.

I was on a late return flight from Los Angeles into Newark, my home hub. I always fly in or out of Newark to LA on the red eye, which lets me arrive during daylight hours. It just so happened for this trip, all the return red eye flights into Newark were booked, meaning I would have to fly all day and land late at night. Spending another night in LA would waste all day Saturday flying back, and I wanted to get home for the weekend. I decided to book that Friday flight back.

The flight was uneventful, and we landed at approximately 10:05 pm in New Jersey. I grabbed my purse and my carry-on bag, then made my way to baggage claim along with the other passengers from my flight.

This one business man pushed his way in next to me as we waited for our luggage. He immediately began to make small talk. I answered his questions but not as eagerly as he asked them. He asked me, what I was doing in LA, whether I was getting a cab, where I lived in New Jersey, and more. He went on to ask what sort of job brought me to LA, did I have a family, and a plethora of other questions that I either mumbled an answer to or ignored completely.

As things sometimes happen, and I often wonder if events happen in a certain sequence to teach us a lesson, our luggage came up last. It was during his insistence to help grab my bags off the luggage carousel, which I reluctantly allowed, that my gut said something here feels seriously wrong; that I felt I was in absolute danger.

As he retrieved his own bags from the carousel, I hurriedly slipped quietly away, headed for the exit and the parking garage to get to my car. I still remember feeling nervous.

As I stepped out into the poorly lit garage, pulling my luggage behind me, I heard a man shout, "HEY!"

It was him. He was walking towards me carrying his backpack and pulling a suitcase.

I ignored him and walked down the sidewalk to the isle where I had parked my car.

He shouted again, "Hey wait, I want to talk to you."

It was then that I slid my hand in my pocket to get my pepper spray and realized that in my rush to get away from him at the luggage carousel, I never stopped and got my pepper spray out of my checked bag. For the first time in this encounter, I was afraid.

I walked faster toward my car, pulling my medium and large suitcases while balancing my carry-on and purse.

He started fast-walking towards me yelling, "WAIT!"

There was not another soul walking around that parking garage, nor car looking for parking. It was eerie.

All I could think of was, I must get to my car, unlock the doors and jump in as fast as I could. I had my keys in my hand because I had kept them zipped in my coat pocket the entire trip to LA and my phone was in the other coat pocket.

I just had to get to my car before him, because he was still coming.

He sounded agitated and kept yelling, "What's wrong with you? I want to talk to you."

As he came closer, I decided to let go of my bags and just get to my car.

Suddenly, like an Angel swooping down to my rescue, car lights flashed and became visible from around the corner. A car slowly moved down the packed isle, its driver apparently looking for parking.

I scrambled back to grab my bags, waved to the approaching driver, and pointed to my car to show the person looking for parking that I was leaving. I threw open my car doors, tossed my bags in the back seat, and jumped in. I immediately locked my doors, started up the car, and backed out.

As I pulled away, I saw the man who had been rushing after me standing between two cars. He stared at me as I passed.

I realized that my hands on the steering wheel were actually shaking. I feel certain to this day I avoided something that could have been tragic.

~ Karen Finocchio, One Tough Muther®, CBS Radio

Reaction and Response

From Karen:

Wow! I can still get emotional when I think of this and how a lifetime of travel and all my habitual safety precautions might have ended badly because this one time I forgot to follow my well-rehearsed, standard travel routine.

To keep this from happening to you or someone you know, please pass the following travel tips around. I hope they make you think twice, take precautions, and help keep you safe.

The first came from my family member, who is a police officer. It is a great tip. If I ever feel threatened like that again in a parking lot or garage, I will do what he advises. It makes TONS of sense.

Tip #1

Always have your phone in your pocket or in your hand if you can carry it. Have your keys and pepper spray in your pocket as well.

If the person threatening you gets close, LEAVE your bags, drop down, and roll under a car or truck. The person pursuing you will not be able to get to you, and you will see them moving from side to side. Then immediately and loudly, call 911. Let them hear you talking to the 911 operator and describe the person as best you can.

ALWAYS, stay under the car until the authorities come, even if you think the person threatening you is gone. You may be wrong, they may be waiting back in hiding. Stay under the car until the police or security comes.

Tip #2

If you are away and must take a taxi, Uber, or car service, be smart and know the route the driver should be taking. You almost certainly have a phone, so use it. And be obvious about it. Google map it, or GPS it, before and while you are in the car.

Always call someone, a family member or a friend, and talk to them while you are in route to your destination. I don't care how late at night it might be, set this up before you go. Tell the person you are talking to where you are, if you are in a taxi or other car service, what you see around you as you are traveling, and the time you should be getting to your destination.

Don't feel the need to talk to the driver, safety should be first.

Traveling alone as a woman can be challenging and a bit intimidating. I hope these tips help you.

Travel safe and remember, if your gut says it feels wrong, it IS!

Subscribe for Free

YOUR Safety
your STORY

Want to share your story?
businesswomansafety.com/yourstory

-10-

At the Heart of the Matter

Are You Making the Mistake of Vulnerability?

In our research, we learned of many victims who believe they have made mistakes or behaved in a way that contributed to their victimization.

Clearly, victims are not to blame for the situation or circumstance that led to their being attacked. Yet many relate feelings of blame and wish they had known beforehand how to avoid situations that led to their being taken advantage of or victimized. Many also believe that, had they known and avoided these practices, their own attack may not have happened.

Be alert to situations that tug at your heartstrings.

Women by nature are sympathetic and nurturing people. It is not right, but it is reality. Victimizers know and use your own natural responses to lure you into their trap.

Avoid appearing to be (or actually being) overly sympathetic or nurturing. By all means, provide help with a broken-down car or flat tire—when you can safely do so. By all means, help the strange man who is wandering the neighborhood calling for his dog to find his pet—when you can safely do so.

We are an open book!

Women tend to give too much information too easily. That's a generality, yet it's also true. In polite conversation, we tell men at bars we are home alone. Or we tell the grocery store bagger and the guy behind us hears that and follows us home. We post on social media that the husband is away, a clear broadcast that puts us at risk if the wrong person sees the post.

It seems like common sense to be careful about what we say about our personal life to strangers or in public situations. Yet, we don't think about it, we don't think about how much we give away in small talk and being polite. Sharing facts can hurt us. Be aware of who you are speaking to and mindful about how much you share!

The Real Story: Office Safety

Is a Peeping Tom a Rapist in Training?

After 20 years with no issues, I was working late one night, busy at my desk, when I noticed I had received a text.

When I opened and read the text, I found a picture of myself seated at my desk, in the very office where I was sitting. It had obviously been taken from the outside looking in through my blinds.

It was so unnerving.

We decided immediately to purchase a camera system for outside. Now, inside my work office, we close blinds at night so we can't be seen.

~ Anonymous Attorney

Reaction and Response

From the Authors:

Is voyeurism like this an act of violence? Should this woman have been afraid? Could this have escalated into dreadful tragedy?

The answer to each of these questions is yes. The people working in this office avoided a bullet, perhaps literally. Their response was to consider this incident as an alert, a warning. They changed the behavior of the individuals directly impacted and made a company-wide policy change.

Arguably, there may be no direct harm in a *Peeping Tom* lurking outside an office window at night observing those inside. The reality is that this lurker escalated from looking to action. He snapped a picture—an act in and of itself a violation of her privacy. THEN, he made the effort to contact her directly to share the picture.

Was his action a threat? In and of itself, possibly not. Yet, if you were in the same situation, would you wait to find out? One hopes not. Protect your privacy as much as reasonably possible in this day of security cameras and cell phone cameras everywhere.

-11-

Realtor Safety

Be Safety-Smart and Business Smart

It goes without saying that meeting in private homes with strangers poses a danger for this profession. After decades of working in this field, we are well-positioned to write a chapter specific to protection for our friends in real estate. We have also gathered input from colleagues and share their tips as well.

Even though this chapter is specifically aimed at real estate professionals, any profession or trade that enters private homes will benefit from this discussion and the safety suggestions. In a world where women are at a physical disadvantage it requires professionals from all walks to be smart, diligent, and crafty in their defense.

Three's Family

From day one, portray yourself as part of a team. Let them know a partner will be with you at the meeting. This will deter any would be predators who hope to lure you alone to a meeting site. This information can be interjected into any meeting conversation and should be known by all involved from the start.

Never take appointments alone, always have a buddy system, a coworker or business colleague who you will do the same for in return. Never take a client for a ride alone from the office, even if during the initial meeting the customer seems professional or safe.

Office Security

If you work from home, never give that address to anyone. If you work out of a professional brokerage, do not meet clients alone in an office, and never take floor time alone. Floor time policy should be discussed with your Broker Owner and safety rules established. If you are the broker owner, it is imperative that you ensure the safety of all your agents with a pro-active security plan.

Personal Marketing

Present a personal image that projects you as a business person. Take care about accepting stranger friendships on personal social media sites that could give information to a would-be perpetrator. If you do not have an office outside of your home, then don't list an address or other personal information in your marketing.

This is vital. Research into how offenders found their victims shows that a big part of the perpetrators ability to locate their victim came from social media information.

Learn how to identify Perpetrators

Usually if your gut tells you something isn't right it isn't. Would be perpetrators will go to great lengths to disguise themselves and present an innocuous and safe face to you. Rapists and murders often study the activities of their victims in great detail, even going so far as to learn their victim's *professional speak* to better lure them to private places to commit their crimes.

The best way to acknowledge this is to be wary of people who present themselves as serious clients but who always want to meet alone. Do not trust this, no matter the situation. No matter how much you believe the person is safe.

Intuition often speaks loudly. If you find yourself in a situation you do not trust, do not proceed. Halt at any intersection, follow your gut, no matter the outcome. Getting the sale is not worth your life.

Dress professionally

Let's face it. In every culture, there are styles of dress that members of the opposite sex will find appealing. While it may not seem provocative to you, there are men who find women's business suits appealing, even a conservative suit with buttoned up blouse and long skirt or slacks. You cannot predict or plan your dress to avoid all appeal to men. At the same time, you can avoid dialing-up the appeal. Dress professionally.

Because this is important and controversial even among women, we address this again, and more fully, in other chapters.

Emergency Word

Develop an emergency communication plan for your team. If you work alone, arrange for a friend to know the plan and be willing to act if necessary. The entire office should know what that code word is. It should be a word not used in everyday conversation, of course.

Create a distress code word that can be texted or said in the event of an emergency. This word should alert your team member that help is needed. By using the distress word, you are able to ask for help without asking, just by interjecting that word.

REALTOR® Safety Checklist

This checklist of safety tips appeared in the online blog, RealtorMag. We think it is a great tool to implement for any real estate professional, indeed any professional who habitually meets clients or prospects in public places. It was developed by Cobra-Defense, a company founded by a veteran law enforcement officer who, in nearly a decade of active service in the streets, fought, arrested, and interviewed hundreds of violent criminals.

The goal behind using this checklist is to reduce the odds of being attacked. Please take the time to review it and implement the recommended practices for yourself and your business associates.

Safety Checklist for Showings

JUNE 2015 | BY JOHN GRADEN

No matter how well you think you know the prospect you're meeting, follow these guidelines when taking them to a property.

The company I work for, Cobra-Defense, was founded by a veteran law enforcement officer who, in nearly a decade of active service in the streets, fought, arrested, and interviewed hundreds of violent criminals. We're built on a background of insight into the minds and actions of bad guys, and there are some common themes regarding how they choose their victims. That information has allowed us to develop a checklist for how to reduce the odds of being attacked.

A lot has been said of the practice of meeting strangers at homes, and it's true that it's not the smartest way to operate. It's been a part of the real estate industry for a long time, and it's not going to change overnight. For agents who will still do it, your office may have a certain protocol around safety that you should follow. This list can be your Agent Safety Protocol, or ASP, to administer in the field. It's based on measures developed by people who have experience working in law enforcement.

Before the Appointment

☑ When you're on the phone setting up an appointment to meet a prospect at a home, tell the prospect that you'll be arriving with a partner. Whether it's true or not, this statement plants the seed that there will be more than one person present—and that's not good news for a criminal.

☑ Arrive at the appointment early, before your client has arrived, and make sure to:
  o Open the windows. If you find yourself needing to make a fast escape but you're not near a door, a window may be your only exit.
  o Unlock all doors. You lose precious time if you have to fiddle with locks to get out.
  o Open the lockbox. The point here is to retrieve the key before your prospect shows up. That way, you won't have to turn your back to him or her to get the key out.

☑ Wait in your car with the doors locked. The danger here is that your car confines you into a small space, but in some cases, the weather dictates that you take shelter. Waiting in the car is still much safer than waiting in the property.

☑ Send a text to your office. Alert someone to where you are and include all the information you have on the prospect. If you need help that person will know pertinent information to give authorities.

☑ Keep your head up. Always be aware of your surroundings. Surprise attacks when you're caught off guard make you more vulnerable.

When the Prospect Arrives

Once your prospective client is in the space with you, pay very close attention to his or her behavior. Small details can clue you in to whether something is wrong:

- ☑ Watch for anything suspicious such as a man wearing a long coat on a hot summer day. He could be concealing a weapon.

- ☑ If it feels like something is awry, trust that feeling and depart ASAP.

- ☑ If everything appears OK at the start, exit your car, but stay well out of arm's reach. The odds of an attack are reduced outside the property rather than inside, but keeping a distance makes it even more difficult for an assailant to jump you.

- ☑ Hold your phone up and say, *"My boss is really strict on safety. Would you please move over to your license plate, so I can send in a photo?"* Quickly take the shots and send them in. Bad guys will probably object, which is your cue to return to your car and leave. Law-abiding citizens will have no problem with it at all.

- ☑ Ask for a photo ID. Take the ID, keeping an arm's length between yourself and the prospect, and then step back a few steps to take a photo of it to send to your office.
    - ○ Ideally, move to the other side of your car so there is a barrier between the two of you while you take the photo.
    - ○ Remember, do not trust or accept anything other than a photo ID. A business card could easily have a fake name, address, and phone number. It's a common practice for criminals to give false in-

formation to mislead and get you to soften your defenses.

☑ Because the lockbox is open and the door already unlocked, say, *"I like clients to enter the home alone as though you were coming home from work. Go ahead. You lead the way."* Give them about 10 seconds of lead time, but not so much that you lose sight of them.

☑ Once you enter the property, keep the prospect in your *10 and 2* [visualize a clock face] range of vision at all times.

☑ Position yourself close to a quick exit as much as you can. However, if your back is to the exit, the bad guy may have a partner who surprises you. Be aware.

☑ Remind the prospect that your partner is on the way. Again, this statement is a huge deterrent.

The key to making this work is to use it consistently. Studies show that it takes 21 to 30 days to develop a new habit. Stick to the ASP for a few weeks, and like most everything in this business, it will become natural to you.

After all, it's your ASP on the line.

CANDY

The Real Story:
Personal Safety

Trust Your Eyes and Instincts

It seemed a normal Friday evening. I browsed the book store, grabbing a few books to preview. I noticed him because he kept slipping out of my line of sight, always a little behind me and off to one side and never more than one bookshelf away.

My taste in reading materials is eclectic, ranging from Science Fiction and Fantasy to Cookbooks, from Mystery to Writing and Computer Books, and from Self-Help to Best Sellers— none of which are in the same sections of the store. Yet, he was consistently browsing the same section that I was in.

He did not approach me, so despite feeling uncomfortable, I relaxed into a cozy chair to read. When I rose to get another book, he was again behind me as I browsed.

This time was different. I stood, pulling books from the shelf and he knelt, no more than two arm's length away.

Suddenly my brain registered what I was seeing from the corner of my eye. (Yes, I kept an eye on him!) He was exposing himself to me! In the middle of the B&N bookstore!

I was horrified and quickly returned to my chair, shaking, uncertain what to do. He did not follow me, and I texted my boyfriend, who was shopping in another store, to come get me-NOW. I didn't feel unsafe. I felt dirty. He had used me in a way I did not agree to or want to be part of.

Then I looked across the room and saw him kneeling again, this time behind a comfy padded arm chair like the one I was in, only this one was occupied by two giggling teenage girls. He knelt on one knee and leaned against the back of their chair, watching them intently. His hand was moving in his groin, inside his unzipped khaki shorts, and I had had enough.

I stood, caught his eye, and deliberately moved to speak to a clerk who was putting away books.

Long story short, he was caught by police in the parking lot attempting to reenter the same B&N later that night after I left. I had given them a good description and snapped his picture before I stood up. I never did have to testify against him, but I would have. He pled guilty and went to jail. I don't believe the teenagers ever knew how he was stalking and using them for his sick gratification, and I am grateful for that.

~ Candy Zulkosky, Author, Writer Coach, Publisher

Reaction and Response

From Candy:

Sometimes, we don't know what to do. I could not have been more surprised by this experience. I questioned what I saw in the book aisle until I saw him doing it again. I never could have predicted his behavior in such a public place.

Should I have gone immediately to the store manager? Perhaps. I was shocked and discounted my own value as a witness. It wasn't until I saw him repeating the same reprehensible behavior with those innocent children that I knew I had to respond.

The lesson here, I believe, is one of staying aware and being prepared to protect yourself and others if need be.

-12-

Keep it Professional

A Revolution is Brewing!

Have you heard? Unless you have been in a cabin in the middle of a forest with no electricity or Internet, then yes. You are aware. The *Me Too* social media movement began with an outpouring of bravado from A-list Hollywood celebrities and kicked off a revolution of women who are fed up and ready to take action.

What's happening?

How about the *Times Up* fund that has gone viral where people across the world donate to help pay legal fees for women who take legal action in cases of sexual harassment and discrimination? Or the incomparable Oprah Winfrey, whose "There is a New Day on the Horizon Ladies" speech was given at the Golden Globes for the Cecil B DeMille award.

Where is it happening?

How about on the covers of People and Time and countless other magazines? Or perhaps closer to home, it's the hair standing up on the necks of men across this nation as women crawl out of the woodwork to speak up, to celebrate, and be heard.

Why is it happening? To begin the healing.

Did the men have it coming? That is a question you may have to answer for yourself. Regardless, there is something to be said for any group of people who feel oppressed and choose to fight back.

We live in a free world which means that the naysayers who think women are exploiting this opportunity are entitled to express their opinion. And there clearly are many who feel that women are jumping on an old bandwagon that should be left alone. There are people who feel women have been given their fair share already; that they have been given enough rights in an ever-evolving society. After all, *they* say, women work amongst us in many male jobs.

What does that mean? What is a male job? A job that was once only occupied by men? Duh. That could be said about every minority too; that their jobs were once held by some other societal caste.

Do we pretend it's old news? That we have more than we deserve?

Do we evolve and demand the same pay for the same job? Do we demand the promotion when deserved?

Do we call out those men who threaten to terminate us for not *playing along*? Do we call out those who offer to elevate us favorably with a price tag of sexual favor?

Do we call out the men who put us at the bottom of the line, in the back of the pile, who dismiss us, who don't listen to our voice?

Yes. Finally, we do. Let's stop worrying—TODAY—about repercussions that finally are being heard in this great nation's court rooms. Let's finally cleanse the souls of outdated workplace rhetoric.

It's time for sexual harassment agreements to be upheld.

It's time that the men around us realize that we are not objects, that we are people, and that intimidation cannot live in the work environment any longer.

Let *Clear Boundaries* be the starting point for every woman who reads it. Wrap your social media profile with the *Keep it Professional* frame. Come together and say, "We will not stand for it."

The Real Story: Violation of Trust

When You Least Expect it...

I have been an event coordinator for a few decades. I've experienced or heard about all kinds of traumatic situations people encounter when traveling and attending events away from home.

Recently, I was completely shocked when someone I was close to in a working relationship stole something right out of my purse. Did I say shocked? Yes. I was shocked and also a bit traumatized.

I now carry a deeper purse, which makes it harder for someone to slip their hand in and take something out. I keep it zipped up. Items like a cell phone or wallet I zip into one of the side pockets. I keep as much as possible out of sight.

How often do you have your purse open sitting beside you? We don't expect that the person next to us, a person we KNOW even casually, will steal. I learned the hard way that there are people out there who we think of as good people who know how to steal quietly! ~Suzi Nelson, Event Coordinator

Reaction and Response

From the Authors:

Take inventory. Stop right now and list everything that's in your purse or wallet without looking. Once you're done, check your list against what's in there. What did you forget?

We carry around items that we don't use often, then if we have to remember what we were carrying, it's nearly impossible. Don't rely on your memory, which is likely to be faulty under the best of circumstances. Instead, make copies—front and back—of everything you carry that is important or that you would have to identify to replace. Leave the copies locked safely away at home so if you have to account for missing items you'll know exactly what they are.

Thieves steal because it's an opportunity to make a little extra cash. Don't make it convenient for them. Ultimately, nothing will stop a determined thief. The harder you make it for them, the more likely a thief is to move on to another target.

-14-

Taking the *Bull* out of Bullying

Are Discrimination and Sexual Discrimination the Same Thing?

So many types of behavior fall under the title of bullying. Even the behaviors surrounding bullying and discrimination are gray and emotional and hard to debate. One constant in this debate that holds true is that Sexual Discrimination can't be placed under the bully title any longer.

Is it bullying behavior when females are insulted in jest, or talked about amongst a circle of male counterparts? Is it bullying when women are laughed at because they say things that sound female minded (whatever that means)?

Yes. When it is women who are being demeaned because of their gender, it is discrimination; it is sexual discrimination. It is also bullying because bullying behavior and discrimination are not mutually exclusive, they can happen at the same time and separately. And can happen with and without a gender bias attached.

Often bullies consider their behavior as a joke or teasing. There is a boundary to be defined here for all people, not only for women.

When comments, whether made in jest or otherwise, make the target of the comment uncomfortable, then that behavior must be looked at, evaluated, and a decision made whether a change in attitude and behavior is necessary.

The lines of delineation around what constitutes bullying and discrimination are currently under a strong microscope, both by societal standards and employers at large. While companies scurry to protect themselves, and release their Sexual Harassment and Discrimination trainings, and check off those boxes for potential legal oversight audits, they will have a hard time burying the past decades of clear and blunt violations that fall under this controversial category.

What is Bullying in the Workplace?

Bullying is a growing and legitimate concern for organizations. While it may feel as though you have returned to high school with the general behavior of individuals casting these aspersions on you, the truth is bullying can lead to resentment—there is nothing juvenile about it. The stress related to bullying and mounting resentment can lead to disgruntled employees, job turn over, and legal action.

Avoid being placed in a position of either being bullied or being accused of being a bully. Stay clear of gossiping in the workplace. Do not participate in hurtful exchanges with coworkers for the sake of putting down another individual. Managers should thwart these types of conversations if overheard.

Individuals who believe that bullying is happening to you or to other employees must report it.

Have you witnessed bullying? Don't commiserate with the victim. Don't ignore it. Report it to human resources.

By arming yourself with clear definitions, you can understand better how to interpret and react to violations should you see it happen, or if it happens to you. Aside from of your employment and rights as an employee of any company, you have the right to respect and fair treatment afforded every human being.

What is Sexual Discrimination?

As defined by the Equal Employment Opportunity Commission (EEOS), sexual discrimination is:

- Unwelcome sexual advances, requests for sexual favors, and other verbal or physical conduct of a sexual nature when:
  - o Submission to such conduct is made either explicitly or implicitly a term or condition of an individual's employment, or
  - o Submission to or rejection of such conduct by an individual is used as a basis for employment decisions affecting such individual, or
  - o Such conduct has the purpose or effect of unreasonably interfering with an individual's work performance or creating an intimidating, hostile, or offensive working environment.

Unwelcome Behavior is the critical word. Unwelcome does not mean *involuntary*. A victim may consent or agree to certain conduct and actively participate in it even though it is offensive and objectionable. Therefore, sexual conduct is unwelcome whenever the person subjected to it considers it unwelcome. Whether the person in fact initially welcomed a request for a date, sex-oriented comment, or joke is—considering all the circumstances—irrelevant when or if the situation become unwelcome.

What is Acceptable, Consensual Behavior?

The Equal Employment Opportunity Commission (EEOC) defines consensual as:

1. When you consensually agreed to the actions that took place between two employees.
2. When, just prior to the sexual statements, you engaged in the same language and banter between the same two parties.

What is Non-Consensual Behavior?

- When you clearly state that you do not like the actions or words of the perpetrator, or coworker in this situation.
- When you have stated NO to an action or asked the individual to cease a conversation that makes you feel uncomfortable.

Individuals feeling violated either verbally or physically, or intimidated to act, or threatened to act should report these actions immediately.

You may also request a session with your HR confidentially to discuss whether something you experienced was a violation. You do not have to discuss the situation with your superior although you should be able to report it if necessary in a private meeting.

You should not gossip or discuss your situation with peers prior to speaking to human resources.

It is important to create and make public your own clear boundaries. We suggest you display your copy of the *Clear Boundaries* book (or a photocopy of the cover, in color!) in your work cubicle as an outward sign to men that you want to *Keep it Professional*.

We hope that this provides an opportunity to show your working world that you are armed with the information, knowledge, and commitment of a well-protected woman.

Eric

The Real Story:
It's Not Your Fault...

but it IS Your Problem

As a former police officer who transitioned into the business world, I may be hypersensitive to the dangers that exist today.

As my daughter says, "Dad, it is not my fault you saw bad things as a cop."

And my response is always, "No, it is not, but it is your problem."

I believe that given today's business and social climate, mental preparation is the single best way to protect yourself. Mental preparation can be the difference between survival and panic.

Living in a mental 'condition white' (as we call it), or a 'this could never happen to me' mindset may be the quickest way to become a victim.

By no means should we walk around paranoid. I would suggest that in today's word we should all be in mental 'condition yellow', a mindset of conscious preparedness.

This puts us in a state of mind that has hoped for the best and planned for the worst. In 'condition yellow', we are alert to the possibilities of what could happen. More often than not, being in a 'condition yellow' mindset will allow us to avoid becoming a victim of a crime.

~ Eric Sachs Co-founder Breakthroughbroker.com
Former Fort Collins Police Services Colorado 13 years

Reaction and Response

From the Authors:

Your intuition is there for a reason. Never ignore it.

Be prepared and in the moment, even in social settings. Your alertness can be compromised for various reasons. For example, the consumption of alcoholic beverages creates an obvious compromise for anyone. Less apparent is how we let our guard down at events and when we are tired.

Maintain the heightened sense of awareness that this book offers.

At the same time, do not let fear rule you. Embrace your life and learn from tools like *Clear Boundaries.* Arm yourself with common sense and awareness against potential dangers.

Throughout this book, the theme of being *mindful, aware, and alert* has repeated among the experts, the victims, and the passionately interested story tellers who have shared their experiences and provided tips. Eric Sachs, as a former police officer, knows well how victims lost their battles or won them. His advice speaks to the difference between blind knowledge and forward alertness. Those perspectives can be the difference between seeing something as it happens or reacting in a moment of debilitating shock.

Eric Sachs now runs an organization filled with both female and male professionals in real estate. Real Estate professionals suffer violent attacks or murders in statistically higher proportions than many other careers, simply by the need for individuals to meet in private home space. Awareness of the violence and risk have changed the face of real estate forever and brought to light real safety concerns. Wise real estate professionals track home showings with electronics, key systems, and buddy systems.

Eric Sachs represents his community, his profession, and the public at large, as a leader and in creating a safe environment for his employee base. As such, we are sincerely grateful for his story that provides a binding to cement the theme throughout this book.

-15-

Closing Remarks

Christine

I thank Jessica Peterson for being fierce, for leading the charge in an ideology I had in my head for a long time. I am grateful for the passion we both feel for women's safety. I am grateful that I posted a women's safety video online. I am grateful Jessica found that video and reached out to ignite the spark of this collaboration.

When I reflect on the number of times I have used my safety training over the course of a 30-year career; when I read the stories shared in this book—Jessica and Candy's stories, those from coworkers, peers, and business professionals—I am awestruck by how seriously dangerous our world has become.

It's hard to imagine the kind of violence that takes a life and yet I have borne witness to two murders. I am pleased beyond measure, to know that my friend Nikki Ann Evangelous, from over 25 years ago, is forever memorialized by this book, along with my coworker and more recent victim, Colleen Brownell.

This book, this gift of safety for women, is a legacy. My hope is for *Clear Boundaries* and this movement to continue long after I am gone to save the lives of women who would otherwise fall to harm.

Jessica

Thank you to every person who invested in this book because you have invested in your own safety. I applaud you for taking steps to be informed and aware around the topic of safety.

A BIG thank you to Christine for saying YES to write this book with me. It has been a lot of work (and fun!) to get it completed. Thank you to Candy for being the amazing editor and publisher. Without the team work this book would not be here.

Thank you to each contributor. I look forward to hearing from more women so we can educate others.

I believe in the ripple effect. My goal is to play a small part in starting a big movement. At my company, we are all about creating stronger relationships, growing companies, and enriching lives in communities and on a global basis.

Thank you to each company that brings this topic into your workplace. It shows you are a caring company and want to protect each person!

Are you ready to pay it forward and share *Clear Boundaries* and this message about safety on social media so other women can become educated and prepared to be safer?

Christine and Jessica

Most of all, we are proud of and grateful for all the women who stepped up and told their personal stories of harm and hurt and who were willing to put their names to it, emphasizing the profound plague that currently exists in this world.

We believe that this book, when read and acted upon as intended, will evoke emotion in as many men as it does women. We believe, *and our experience has proven this, even before publication,* that men want to be a part of our movement; that male bosses and business owners want to support our efforts to move the needle forward in a profound way.

We applaud every man who is as brave as our women to stand up. Our greatest growth as a country, as humans, occurs when people comes together to evolve. We believe this is happening and are proud to be small stars in the universe of human progress and growth.

This book has been a pleasure to write. We wish everyone who reads it the very best in their professional quest, their many travels, and their journey to higher ground and safer living.

We want to thank those women and men who made anonymous contributions to the book. They must be faceless in protection of their brand because of the stereotype and rhetoric that still exists and that can be damning to their professions or businesses.

A sad commentary, but kudos to the smart women who recognize that even an anonymous voice has more power than silently standing by. These quiet heroines deserve recognition. Their stories in this book are real. Their contributions are given by people who have experienced and survived the essential safety issues at the heart of this book. We are grateful indeed.

Lives cannot be replaced. There is no such thing as too safe.

Be your own advocate.

Be your own guard dog.

Be aware.

Be alert.

Be SAFE!

-16-

The Gift of Safety

Truly it Keeps on Giving

Will you consider giving the Gift of Safety? Like you and many others, we watch in growing alarm as year after year the rate of violence against women continues to rise. We have decided that enough is enough. With this book we take action. And we invite you to join us—to act.

This book is written for the world we live in today and offers safety tips that are practical and relevant. *Clear Boundaries* has put what women need into one handy manual that gives every woman real knowledge. We have gathered data, tips, and instruction from experts in the field of business travel, self-defense and hired protection. We have included shared, real-life stories from leading business women in America. In one impactful high-speed manual, you have the tactics to protect yourself. We salute you for picking up this book and reading it. Is reading this book enough for you?

What price would you pay to protect your loved one?

Pretty much anything? We already know that's likely to be your answer. You, as do we, know many who have faced tragedy and would do anything to gain back that opportunity to protect and who sadly have no second chance.

What if our best defense is for EACH of us to have the knowledge to act in the moment of our own dangerous intersections?

What if you could thwart a potential conflict or perilous situation by planning ahead of time how to handle such encounters?

Clear Boundaries is the answer to both of these scenarios!

Proactively protect those you care about from the growing threats society presents towards females every day, both virtually and physically. Grab another copy of *Clear Boundaries: Every Business Women's Essential Guide to Safety.*

Give this handbook and manual, created for women by women, to those you care for and about.

Give the Gift of Safety and show others that they matter! That they are loved! Tell them that you care enough to help them stay safe.

Give the Gift of Safety. Buy another copy of this book and gift it to a friend. Ask your company to buy a copy for your office library.

Tell your public relations and human resources departments that you want Christine or Jessica to deliver a training or come as keynote speakers for the next corporate all hands event.

We ask that all women take their images seriously, their posts seriously, their interactions seriously, and that they understand they can't tolerate or create blurred lines any longer. Let's hold ourselves accountable. Let's refuse to allow others control over our safety.

Jessica Peterson

Jessica is a best-selling author of five books and a featured co-author in three others. After a 20-year career in banking and finance, Jessica stepped into her dream and created a Social Media agency to provide a positive impact for the businesses she served and for their clients. Jessica knows is a Connector, Supporter, and Protector.

She has collected many accolades, including awards for top sales, top employee, and more. In 2015 she had the honor of being a TEDx speaker in Colorado. She is a certified 100k Impact Business Coach.

After many years of experience and testing social media, Jessica developed a proprietary plan of action to grow your business on social media. She used this simple plan to grow an affiliate team of over 3,000 sales associates worldwide in only one year and was selected as top speaker and trainer out of 260,000 people.

After personally encountering frightening and dangerous situations, she knew this book must be published to protect other women; especially the younger generation entering the workforce. With her social media experience, she has vital tips and tools to share about safety!

Christine Beckwith

From a modest start three decades ago in the teller line of a small Massachusetts-based credit union, Christine rose through the ranks of mortgage sales from processing to origination, branch management, and eventually district, regional, and national management.

In doing this she has become a sought-after public speaker on the topics of real estate finance and business planning and today travels the country educating real estate and mortgage finance professionals both in and out of AnnieMac Home Mortgage.

She is a decorated sales veteran, having won sales contests at every level in multiple markets.

Christine has experienced first-hand many scary moments in the corporate world. She barely escaped one from a coworker badly beaten. A book about safety for women has long been on her mind to create and get out to the world.

Acknowledgements

We would like to offer a truly special thank you to everyone who participated in making this book a success. In particular, we thank and acknowledge the assistance of these individuals:

- Jessica M. Farrelly, Icard, Merrill, Cullis, Timm, Furen & Ginsburg, P.A.
- Christine Sensenig Hultman Sensenig + Joshi

Subscribe for Free

YOUR Safety
your STORY

Want to share your story?
businesswomansafety.com/yourstory

Made in the USA
Middletown, DE
08 January 2019